# TRAINING TREE
## *for Riders*

AMANDA J. BERGES

TRAINING TREE FOR RIDERS
Copyright 2012 by Amanda Berges

All rights reserved. No part of this book may be used or reproduced in any manner whatsoever, including electronic media, internet, or newsletters, without written permission from the publisher, except in the case of brief quotations embodied in critical reviews. For permission, write to Alpine Publications, Inc., P O Box 7027, Loveland, CO 80537.

ISBN 13: 978-1-57779-124-9
ISBN 10: 1-57779-124-X

The information contained in this book is complete and accurate to the best of our knowledge. All recommendations are made without guarantee on the part of the author or Alpine Publications, Inc. The author and publisher disclaim any liability with the use of this information.

For the sake of simplicity, the terms " he" or "she" are sometimes used to identify an animal or person. These are used in the generic sense only. No discrimination of any kind is intended toward either sex.

Cover Design, Charts and Graphs: Laura Newport
Editing: Dianne Nelson
Layout: Shadow Canyon Graphics
Photographs by the author unless otherwise noted.
Illustrations: Mary-Lynn Jones, Pretty Bird Studio

First printing 2012

1 2 3 4 5 6 7 8 9 0
Printed in the United States of America.

# Acknowledgments

Thanks to all of my models, including those horses and riders from Double Deuce Farm in Concord, Swampy Oak Farm in Andover, and Lake Erie College Equine Studies Program in Painesville, Ohio.

Thanks to Mary-Lynn Jones of Pretty Bird Studio for being incredibly easy to work with, never taking offense when I wanted to change some detail of her artwork, and being a prompt, professional and lovely artist.

Thanks to Meredith Manor International Equestrian College for the use of their training tree illustration.

Thanks to friend and riding instructor Megan Carl for being brilliant, both as an equestrienne and as an editor.

Thanks to Grace Butcher for being the voice of reason throughout the project. You came into my life with fortuitous timing, and now I feel like I've known you forever.

Thanks to Dianne Nelson and Emily McHenry for editing.

Thanks to all of my riding instructors, four-legged and two-legged, and specifically to Sylvia Wilson for showing me the effectiveness of using a polo wrap on the saddle and Chuck Kinney for demonstrating a cure for rocking shoulders at the canter.

Thanks to the Ultimate Dressage Bulletin Board for being the ultimate resource for anything, no matter how obscure, horse-related or not.

Thanks to all of my students, four-legged and two-legged, who have taught me how to teach.

# Contents

INTRODUCTION . . . . . . . . . . . . . . . . . . . . . . . . . . . . . . . . . . . . . . . . . . . 1

**Chapter 1**: LONGEING . . . . . . . . . . . . . . . . . . . . . . . . . . . . . . . . . . . 9
   Equipment   11
   Technique   15
   Sensitizing, Desensitizing   16
   Lessons   18
   To Use or Not Use Stirrups   21
   On Your Own   21

**Chapter 2**: RELAXATION . . . . . . . . . . . . . . . . . . . . . . . . . . . . . . . 23
   Focused Relaxation   29
   Posture and Relaxation   33
   On Your Own   35
   Moving On   35

**Chapter 3**: BALANCE . . . . . . . . . . . . . . . . . . . . . . . . . . . . . . . . . . 37
   Vertical Balance   37
   Lateral Balance   46
   On Your Own   49

**Chapter 4**: RHYTHM . . . . . . . . . . . . . . . . . . . . . . . . . . . . . . . . . . 53
   Walk   53
   Trot or Jog   56
   Canter or Lope   58
   The Training Bush   61
   On Your Own   61

**Chapter 5**: FITNESS . . . . . . . . . . . . . . . . . . . . . . . . . . . . . . . . . . . 63
   On Your Own   68

**Chapter 6**: SUPPLENESS . . . . . . . . . . . . . . . . . . . . . . . . . . . . . . . 69
   Setting Ground Poles and Cavalletti   71
   Sitting the Trot   72
   On Your Own   74

**Chapter 7:** FEEL . . . . . . . . . . . . . . . . . . . . . . . . . . . . . . . . . . . . . . . . . . 79
    Feel Through the Seat   80
    Feel Through the Reins   81
    On Your Own   85

**Chapter 8:** INFLUENCE . . . . . . . . . . . . . . . . . . . . . . . . . . . . . . . . 87
    Influence Through the Seat   87
    Influence Through the Reins   90
    On Your Own   95

**Chapter 9:** POSITION: A Means to an End . . . . . . . . . . . . . . . . . . 97
    Order of Progression   99
    Form Equals Function   100
    On Your Own   101

**Chapter 10:** OFF THE LONGE . . . . . . . . . . . . . . . . . . . . . . . . . . 103
    Restructuring the Tree   103
    The Horse   106
    On Your Own   107

**Chapter 11:** WARM-UP AND EVALUATION . . . . . . . . . . . . . . . . 109
    Guideline #1: Have a Plan   109
    Guideline #2: Locate and Inspect the Foundation   111
    On Your Own   112

APPENDIX 1: LESSON PLANS . . . . . . . . . . . . . . . . . . . . . . . . . . . . . . 115
   First Mounted Lesson, Beginning Rider   115
   Second Mounted Lesson, Beginning Rider   116
   Third Mounted Lesson, Beginning Rider

APPENDIX 2: SKILLS COMMONLY DEVELOPED CONCURRENTLY . . . . . . 118

ABOUT THE AUTHOR . . . . . . . . . . . . . . . . . . . . . . . . . . . . . . . . . . . . 119

INDEX . . . . . . . . . . . . . . . . . . . . . . . . . . . . . . . . . . . . . . . . . . . . . . 120

# Introduction

Countless trainers look to a training scale, training "tree," or training pyramid as one guide in the development of their young horses. It provides a framework to follow; not as specific as a map, but more like a compass to point the trainer in the right direction. It can also be of help in determining where the weaknesses lie in the training of a "problem" horse. Although there are several slightly different versions of training scales, a common one is as follows:

1. Relaxation
2. Rhythm
3. Contact
4. Impulsion
5. Straightness
6. Collection

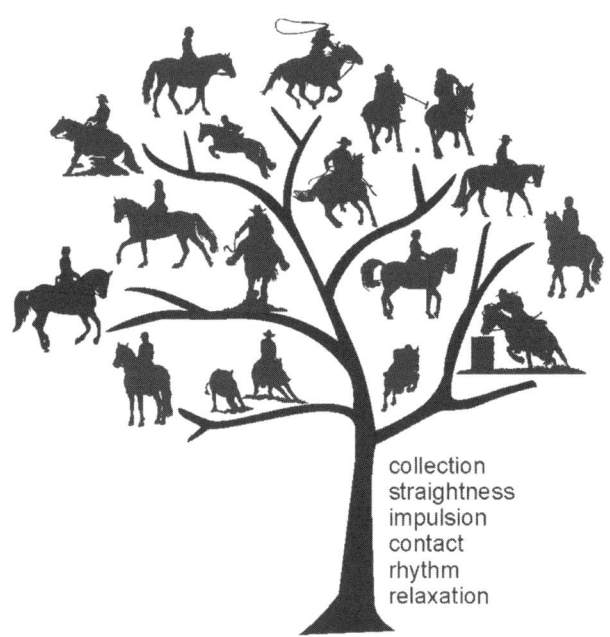

The training tree/scale is the recognized path to all disciplines for any horse.

2  *Training Tree for Riders*

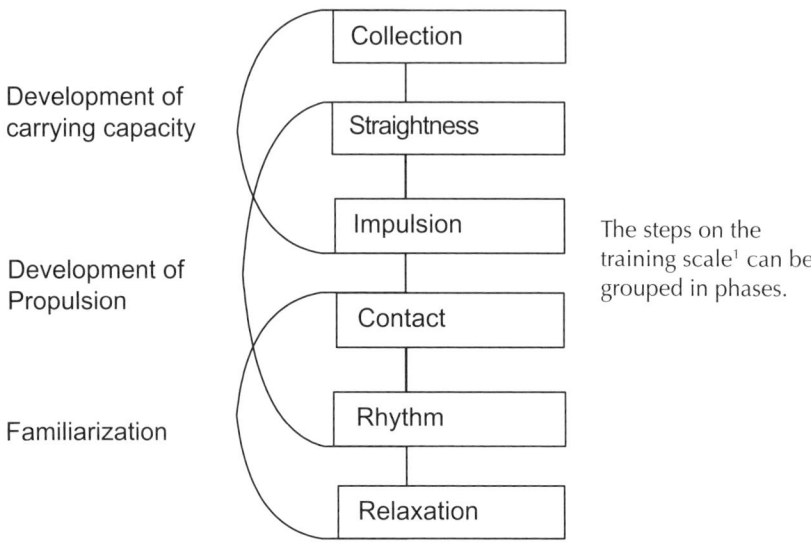

The steps on the training scale[1] can be grouped in phases.

Steps can be combined into phases. The first phase, focusing on familiarizing the horse with his job of carrying the rider, encompasses rhythm, relaxation, and contact with the bit. The second phase overlaps the first to include contact, impulsion, and straightness; it develops the horse's strength and ability to move with propulsion. The third phase overlaps again to include impulsion, straightness, and collection, and it develops the horse's ability to bear weight efficiently.

Regardless of discipline, a young horse must progress through all of these steps and phases before he can be expected to develop skill in specialized training. For this reason, some people prefer to visualize the training scale in the form of a tree, where the stages progress up the trunk and the many branches represent the training specialties (as shown on the preceding page). In addition to reminding us of the building blocks that must be in place before we progress to more advanced skills in the horse's overall training, the training tree also serves as a reminder of qualities that must be established in our warm-up *every day* before we progress to more advanced skills within that session. Such a versatile tool, and yet so simple!

# INTRODUCTION 3

Anyone who has trained a horse knows that the stages are not clear-cut; in fact, there can be considerable overlap, as is illustrated by the phases mentioned above. Steps blur and run together. Still, the training tree is a useful tool—one that has withstood the test of time since it was first published in the 1912 *Heeresdienstvorschrift* (or *HDV*), the German military guide by General von Redwitz and Colonel von Heydebreck. It has been included in subsequent editions of the *Heeresdienstvorschrift*, as well as in the popular *Official Instruction Handbooks of the German National Federation*.[1] A slightly different version has been adopted by the United States Dressage Federation. The training tree is most familiar to dressage riders; however, it was designed for use with all horses regardless of specialty. The figure below shows this beautifully in a graphic designed by Ron Meredith and used as an instructional aid at Meredith Manor.

This version of the training tree was designed by Ron Meredith to illustrate the teachings at Meredith Manor. © 2011 Meredith Manor International Equestrian Centre.

---

1, 1. *The Training Scale* by Dr. Thomas Ritter, Topline Ink , 2009.

## 4  Training Tree for Riders

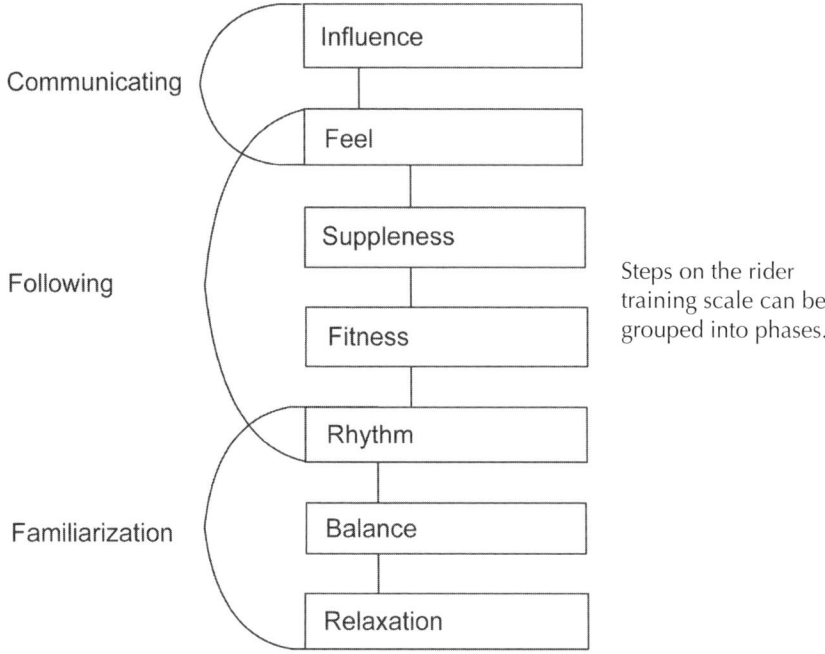

Steps on the rider training scale can be grouped into phases.

The goal of this book is to provide and explain a similar training scale for the development of the rider. As with the equine version, it is intended to give direction in the training of a new student, to assist in uncovering weaknesses in the rider's education that interfere with further advancement of skills, and to offer a checklist for the daily warm-up of advanced riders. Also, again as with the equine version, I am quite certain that others will propose different terms with which to label the steps or slightly alter the order of progression. My hope is that more thought will be given to the rider's early education, that a more systematic approach than is generally used will become common, that frustration will be reduced for both students and teachers, and that the holes that are all too common in the education of our nation's riders will shrink in size and lessen in number.

The purpose of correct gymnastic training of the horse is to allow him to perform with complete relaxation, suppleness, and flexibility. If the horse is not rhythmic, forward, straight, and softly accepting the rider's communication through the bit, his training cannot be considered correct no matter what movements or tricks he can execute. Similarly, the goal of training riders is to enable them to perform with complete relaxation, suppleness, and flexibility. If riders are not balanced, supple, fully aware of the movement of the horse underneath them, and able to respond appropriately, their training cannot be considered correct, no matter the size of the jumps they can clear or other tricks they can perform. The purpose of basic training in both cases is to produce the kind of horse-and-rider team that is universally accepted as being beautiful to see: graceful, fluid, balanced, and performing tasks with lightness and ease. Most instructional systems focus on teaching tasks. The rider training tree focuses on teaching the qualities that prevent those tasks from being performed as tricks—qualities that will be transferable to any horse and any style of riding.

The Rider Training Tree reminds us that solid basic training
is a prerequisite to all equestrian disciplines.

## OF RIDERS, HORSES, AND HOUSES

The training tree is, by definition, a tool for basic training. But don't be fooled—it is of utmost importance for the trainer of advanced students as well. Too often, riders struggle year after year toward the same elusive goals and still experience the same difficulties and the same roadblocks. Too often, horses are ridden with bigger spurs and stronger bits when their riders encounter difficulties. In both situations, the solution to the problem is to go back to whatever was missed in that individual's education. Like a building that is unsteady, the builders must back up to the solid portions and rebuild from there.

Horses and riders can give the illusion of being trained to a fairly advanced level, when in reality, important components are missing or insufficient. This may only become apparent when the horse or rider is asked for work of a much higher level of difficulty. This situation can be compared to a weak building foundation: depending on the extent of the weakness, the foundation may crumble immediately when any sort of load is placed on it. In that case, the problem is easy to identify and, while frustrating, is relatively easy to repair. With a less obvious weakness, the carpenter may proceed with construction unaware of the problem. It may happen that the first floor goes up just fine, but with the addition of the second floor, the foundation gives out. Still, it is a clear-cut problem, but now the solution is much more frustrating and much more costly. It could happen that the foundation is strong enough to support the house to completion. However, over months, and maybe years, the doors and windows will become difficult or impossible to open and close properly. Plumbing may even spring leaks. The problem at this point is extremely costly to solve, if it is even identified!

Similarly, the training of horses can progress in spite of a weak foundation. These are often the horses who suddenly cease to progress at a particular level after having made rapid progress to that point. They may be horses whose soundness fails them at an early age due to the stresses placed on their bodies to perform at a level for which they were not adequately prepared. Or they may be the horses who are labeled "difficult," "resistant," or so many other terms, who are actually incapable of doing what is asked of them due to lack of proper preparation. Therefore, it is frequently the trainers of advanced-level horses who are most familiar with the principles of the equine training scale, for it is they who must contend with the consequences when the scale is not adhered to, and it is they who reap the benefits when it is.

With riders, we talk about the "basics." But as with horses and houses, a rider can progress to quite an advanced level in some cases before deficiencies result in a cessation of progress, or worse, injury. Often the horse is blamed for the problems, when in fact the horse is only hobbled by the limitations of the rider. Instructors of beginning riders can and should instill the basics into their students, but instructors of advanced riders must be prepared in case the students do not possess the basics. They must be able to identify the core reasons for problems that are seemingly unrelated to one another or to basic work, and to develop an individualized program that will reinforce the riders' foundation. At the very least, instructors of advanced riders should be prepared to teach feel (Chapter 7) in addition to the advanced techniques in their area of expertise. Feel is commonly (and mistakenly) considered a skill that is intrinsic to a few lucky individuals and cannot be taught; therefore, many riders may not have learned to feel the horse's movement.

Some people balk at the idea of focusing on the basics. They want to get to the "good stuff" and leave behind what they perceive as the time-consuming repetition of tedious drills. But truly, there is no reason why the basics can't be fun, interesting, challenging, and rewarding. Without a doubt, attention to the basics will allow riders to realize their goals *much more quickly* than they could any other way. In this age of instant gratification, it is important to instill these basic qualities in riders as quickly and efficiently as possible. By starting with a comprehensive plan based on the rider training tree for how to instill the basic skills, the best lesson plans become even more efficient.

## ON YOUR OWN

An important difference between riders and either horses or houses is the ability of riders to contribute to their own development.

It is undeniably important for riders to get themselves in front of a qualified instructor regularly. If you have the opportunity to ride in between lessons, then practicing the exercises described in this book can only help with your progress. If lessons are not as frequent as you would like, a friend may be interested in partnering with you. The two of you may help one another in your progress by sharing observations, making suggestions, longeing one another on your horses, and/or manning a video camera. *If most of your work must be done alone, please read the Chapter 10, "Off the Longe," first.*

Video recording is a tool that should be used generously. No matter how vividly an onlooker describes what you or your horse is doing, there is nothing quite like seeing for yourself. For example, it often feels to students who are learning the use of the "outside-leg-behind-the-girth" that their heel is somewhere in the vicinity of the horse's tail, when in fact it has barely moved from its original location. Riders who habitually slouch feel straight when they are far from it. Video can help to enlighten the rider as to what is actually happening, and subsequent tapes can reveal and reinforce progress.

The Rider Training Tree can and should be used by riders seeking to solidify their foundations on their own or with the help of a friend. In many of the following chapters, readers will find tips for such riders in the sections entitled "On Your Own."

# CHAPTER 1

# LONGEING

The rider's training scale may be utilized most effectively in lessons on the longe. Longeing has long been recognized as the best way to start new riders and the most effective way to develop a good seat. At the Spanish Riding School in Vienna, new students generally spend at least two years on the longe. Riders must learn to follow the horse's movement before they can influence that movement effectively. Longeing allows riders to concentrate on feeling and following without needing to concern themselves with pace, direction, or quality of gaits. This simplification of focus streamlines the learning process. It becomes more efficient and therefore faster.

Longe lessons are good for the horse, too. The instructor gives the "aids" so that the horse is relieved from the frustration of trying to distinguish between aids from the rider and uncoordinated bumps. (The rider does not apply aids until she has developed sufficient coordination and bodily control to do so with clarity.) Longeing preserves the sensitivity of the horse's mouth, because there is no possibility of the rider balancing on the reins if she has none. Thus, your carefully trained horse maintains both his responsiveness to the aids and his cheerful goodwill!

Another consideration is that, when the rider's initial education is not via the longe, and if she chooses to advance beyond a very basic level of riding, she must relearn many things. A typical "beginner's horse," safe and plodding, gives a very different feel from a more advanced horse. The rider must learn anew how to ride each gait, because it feels very different to ride gaits that are forward, engaged, and "through." A rider taught on the longe can learn from the outset what correct movement feels like, so again, the process is streamlined, and an educated rider emerges sooner.

Of course, in order to teach a rider on the longe, a good longe horse must be available along with an instructor who has good longe technique. A qualified longe horse can be created from nearly any riding horse provided the horse is sound, not overly sensitive and that he has tolerable gaits. The process of creating the longe horse requires little more than the practice of correct longe technique, with careful attention to consistency of gaits and promptness of response. Longe work has a calming, steadying influence on the horse when it is done well; therefore, even a horse that might be too high strung or sensitive to cope with beginning riders off the longe may handle such riders very well on the longe. This will depend heavily on the skill of the instructor: The less experienced he is with training horses on the longe, teaching riders on the longe, or teaching riders in general, the more important it will be for him to use a horse that has natural qualifications, such as a very steady temperament.

To become a qualified longe-er, help from an experienced trainer will be very valuable. Longeing well is as much an art as is riding well. In each case, there is no substitute for direct instruction under a knowledgeable eye when you are learning. Body language is very powerful when you are working a horse on the longe, yet it is a language in which most people are far from fluent. An experienced longeing instructor (that is, someone who teaches how to longe) should be able to interpret both what the new longe-er is communicating, perhaps unintentionally, to the horse, and what the horse is communicating to the longe-er through their respective body positions. A good instructor also should share the finer points of technique. Time spent at this stage will pay excellent dividends. To rush the process increases the potential risk for the student and is therefore unacceptable.

The horse and long-er must work together consistently and flawlessly before a rider is added to the mix. Then, a fairly advanced rider should be utilized—one who will not be upset by unanticipated antics on the part of the horse. The horse must be allowed to become accustomed to the movements required by the various exercises that students might perform. When he scarcely notices even the largest movements, like marching steps and scissors kicks, but maintains rhythm and attention to the instructor, then he may be ready for regular lessons.

# LONGEING 11

## EQUIPMENT

Equipment required for safe and effective longe lessons includes the following:

1. A longe line, or longe rein, of twenty-five to thirty feet in length. Any longer is cumbersome; any shorter and the resultant small circle will make it difficult for students to sit in balance. Instead, they will feel pushed to the outside with every step.

2. A longe cavesson made of leather with a padded brass nosepiece. Those of other materials do not stay in place on the horse's head, nor do they transmit aids via the longe line with nearly the strength or clarity. Be sure to buckle the jaw strap tightly across the jawbone to keep the outside cheek piece out of your horse's eye.

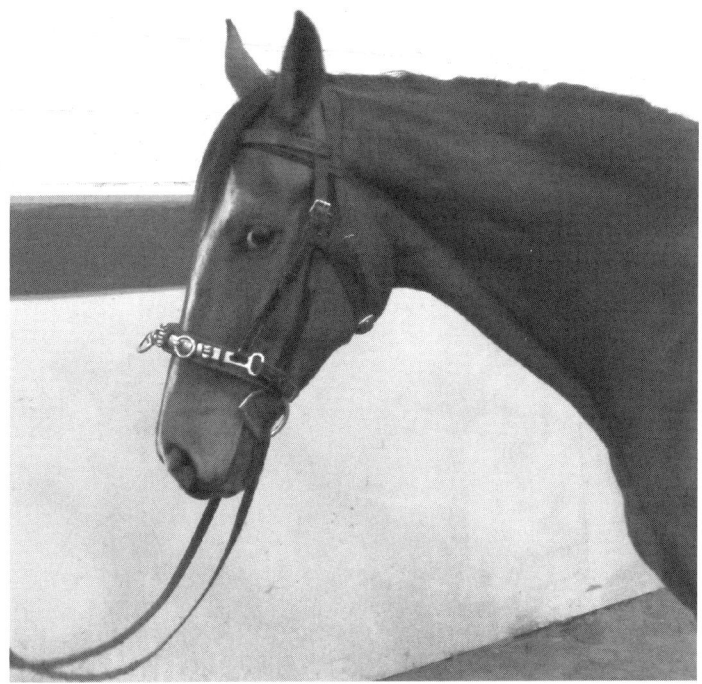

A horse wearing a longeing cavesson over the bridle.

3. A longe whip kept free of knots.

4. Boots for your horse, even if he doesn't usually wear them when he is ridden. Between the constant turning and the potential of the longe line to restrict balancing actions of the head and neck, the chances of the horse knocking himself are increased. Therefore, the front legs, at least, must be protected.

5. A snaffle bridle, preferably with the noseband removed so as not to interfere with the longe cavesson. Reins should be removed or twisted around each other and the throatlatch passed through a loop to secure them.

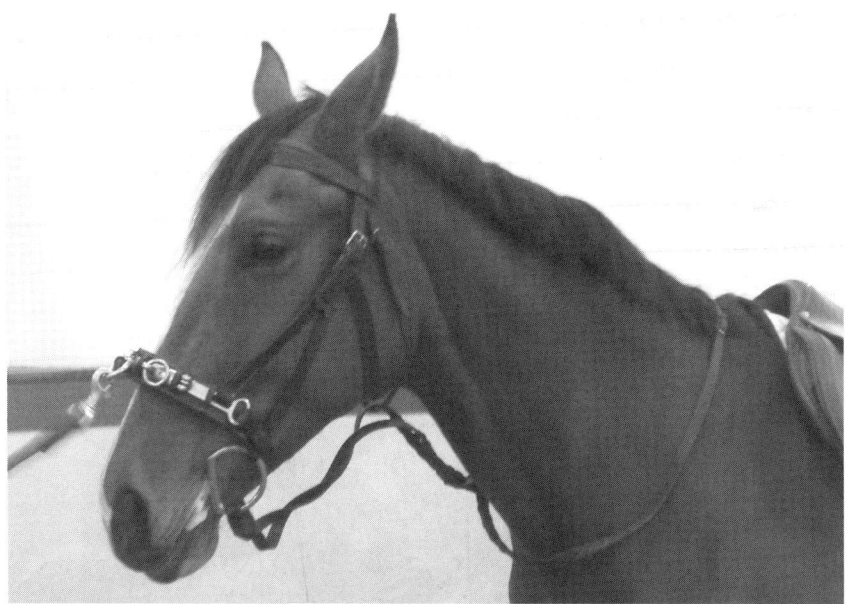

Reins bound up for longeing without a rider.

6. A saddle that fits both horse and rider. Your horse cannot work well if his withers or shoulders are being pinched. Your rider cannot ride well if the saddle is placing her in an awkward or unbalanced position. Be sure that the saddle is level when viewed from the side. The deepest part of the seat should be in the middle. Sometimes saddles appear to fit well until the rider mounts and her weight compresses the padding under the back of the saddle. Don't be fooled!

# LONGEING 13

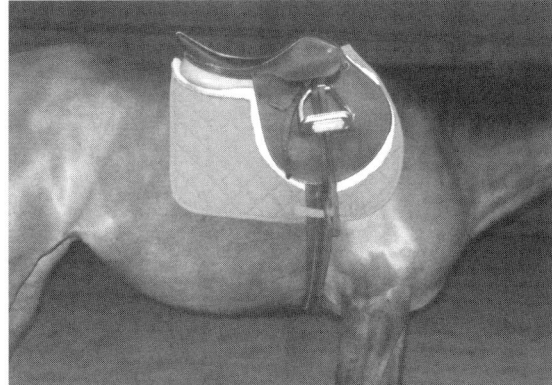

Not a good fit—the saddle is too narrow over the horse's shoulder, causing it to sit too high. The rider will be placed in the back of the saddle, rather than in the center over the stirrup bars, and her legs will persistently slide forward.

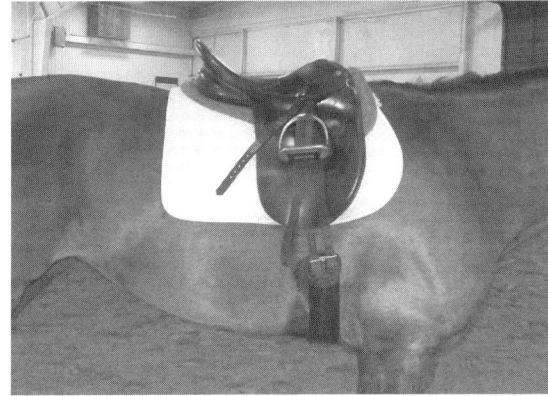

A much better fit.

7. Side reins of leather or nylon, with elastic, rubber donuts, or neither, depending on the preference of the horse and handler. Elastic (the author's preference) is most commonly used for young horses; solid side reins are generally reserved for highly trained horses. Side reins with donuts have some give, although they are less than elastic, and are for in-between levels of training or general use. Unfortunately, they bounce, which is uncomfortable for sensitive horses. Nylon side reins, due to their strength, must have a breakaway feature for safety.

## Side Reins

Side reins are an often-misunderstood piece of equipment. They are not "gadgets" or head-setting devices. They are a legitimate training tool and are accepted and respected by the most classical of trainers. Their place in the tack room is nearly as important as that of the snaffle bridle: you can train a horse or rider without either one or both, but you would be making the job much harder by making that choice.

Of course, any piece of equipment can be rendered useless, or even dangerous, when it is used incorrectly. Side reins must always be attached rather loosely at first, even with an experienced longe horse, and shortened in stages to a length that is appropriate to the horse's conformation and level of training. The height at which the side reins are attached to the girth, billets, or surcingle will also vary according to these criteria but will not need adjusting as frequently. The height is correct if the side reins are horizontal when the horse carries his head in its natural position. The horse should always be encouraged to seek contact with the bit, but if the side reins are too long, the horse will fall on his forehand in his effort to reach the bit. Therefore, they must be shortened until the bit is comfortably within the horse's reach.

On a lesser-trained horse, the side reins will be rather long and low. As the horse's training progresses, the carrying capacity of the hindquarters will increase. The horse will gradually begin to step more deeply under his center of gravity with his hind legs. This will require his pelvis to lower and tuck under, and, as a chain reaction, the rest of his spine will round upward. This will be most noticeable in the raising and arching of the horse's neck, but the change will come very gradually. Often it is first apparent in the fit of the side reins. They may appear too long, too low, or both, and must be adjusted. In this way, side reins support the athletic development of the horse; they don't create it.

It is in this supportive role that side reins are most commonly appreciated; however, it is not their only benefit:

1. They help maintain straightness, by channeling the horse between them.
2. They provide a consistent contact for the horse to stretch into, which promotes consistent gaits and a consistent frame in all gaits and transitions.

Because straightness and consistency are necessary qualities in a longe horse, it logically follows that the longe horse must wear side reins.

## TECHNIQUE

A great deal of what goes into longe technique are subtleties of body language and constant, two-way communication with the horse that must be developed with time and practice. What follows are general directives that will help to promote communication and fruitful practice.

The stance of the longe-er should be similar in many respects to that of the rider: erect, knees slightly bent, balanced over the feet, with a straight line from elbow to hand and down the rein to the horse's mouth. Viewed from above, the longe line, whip, and horse should form the three sides of an isosceles triangle. The longe-er must not walk about while longeing but remain in an area roughly the size of a manhole cover to ensure that the horse describes a true circle. Think of your whip and longe line as the spokes of a wheel. If the hub (the longe-er) gets off center, the wheel will not turn smoothly. The consistency of bend is important for allowing your student to focus on the lesson without the disruption of unexpected shifts in the horse's balance.

For many, the voice is the primary aid for longeing, but it is of limited use in many circumstances. In a busy arena, for example, many voices compete.

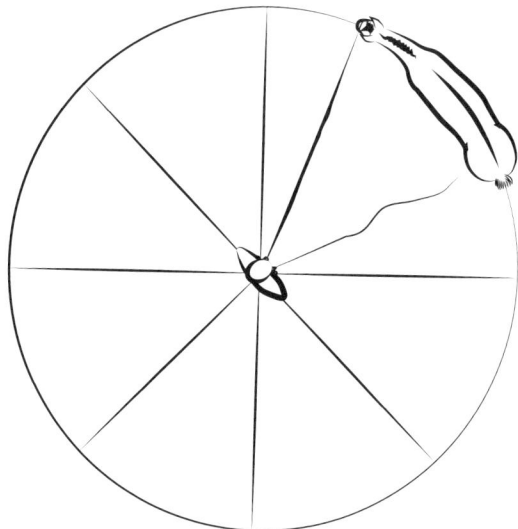

The horse, longe line, and whip form the three sides of a triangle.

In a longe lesson, the instructor's attempts to communicate simultaneously with both the horse and the rider may lead to confusion. To minimize this, it is necessary to use a distinct tone for communicating with the horse. It also helps to clarify commands to the horse if words are drawn out. For example, a short, clipped "trot" can be nearly unintelligible, but if it is drawn out to "trrrrrott," the intent is clear to the horse. Furthermore, the inflection can be varied to indicate energy level. An upward transition from walk to trot is requested by saying "trrrrrOTT," while a downward transition from canter to trot is requested thus: "TRRRRRott." Through these variations, the longe-er can create a clear distinction between words intended for the horse and those directed to the rider.

The whip is an extension of the longer's arm and, as such, clarifies and reinforces her body language. The whip should never be cracked but rather swept toward and away from the horse's hindquarters. The height of the whip may also be used as an aid. Positioning the tip of the whip on the ground and holding it still means halt. Raised just off of the ground, it indicates walk. Raise the whip to between the knee and the waist to indicate trot, or between the waist and the shoulder to indicate canter. Because horses communicate primarily via body language, they are very sensitive to these types of cues and pick them up readily with consistent use.

Combined with distinct tones for verbal commands to the horse, teaching the horse to respect and respond to the height of the whip as an aid frees the instructor to concentrate more fully on the rider. The instructor may, for example, discuss with the student a different gait than the one currently being ridden, without concern that the horse will make an untimely transition to that gait.

## SENSITIZING, DESENSITIZING

If the horse fails to respond to the voice and whip as driving aids, there is nothing wrong with letting him feel the end of the lash on his hindquarters. A gentle touch is all that is required to let the horse know that you are willing and able to reach him and that the whip is to be respected.

If, on the other hand, the horse fears the whip, then you as the handler must relieve his fear. Standing at his head, and holding the lash to prevent any

## LONGEING 17

The whip is held at different heights; it is held at the waist to indicate a trot.

Whip held higher to indicate a canter.

Whip held low to indicate a walk.

unexpected motion, allow the horse to smell and inspect the whip if he will. Proceed to scratch and caress his neck with the whip, then his shoulder, and then the opposite side of the neck and shoulder. Move on from one part of the horse's body to the next only when your horse is rather bored with what you are doing. This may take minutes—or days. With a little patience, you should soon be able to touch the horse anywhere with the whip easily, including on his legs and belly. At that point, release the lash and begin the process again. Be sure to praise the horse at frequent intervals for his bravery! Of course, all such issues—over-sensitivity or under-sensitivity—must be thoroughly settled before the horse is even considered for use in longe lessons.

## **LESSONS**

For the longe lesson itself, the reins should be looped around the horse's neck as shown in the photo on the next page. This is done by placing the reins over the horse's neck as usual, grasping the loop of rein hanging on the far side of the neck, pulling it forward under his chin, and then bringing it up over his head again. In this way, the reins are out of the way but are available to the rider in case of emergency.

    The horse should first be warmed up without the rider. The warm-up should include all of the gaits to be ridden in the lesson and allow the horse to develop the engagement/collection level required for the lesson. The exact amount of time will depend on the needs of the horse as well as on the lesson plan. A lesson consisting entirely of walk will require a different warm-up than will a lesson focusing on the collected canter.

    Side reins should always be removed while the rider mounts, then the horse should be walked a few steps before they are reattached so that the horse has full access to his back muscles as he accepts the rider's weight. The length of the side reins will again depend on the lesson plan. Any time that the horse will be walking for more than a couple of steps the side reins must be lengthened as compared to the normal working length for trot and canter. Otherwise you risk destroying your horse's walk rhythm. Short side reins in walk can also cause the horse to feel "trapped" and explosive behavior may result, with potential for serious injury to both horse and rider.

# LONGEING 19

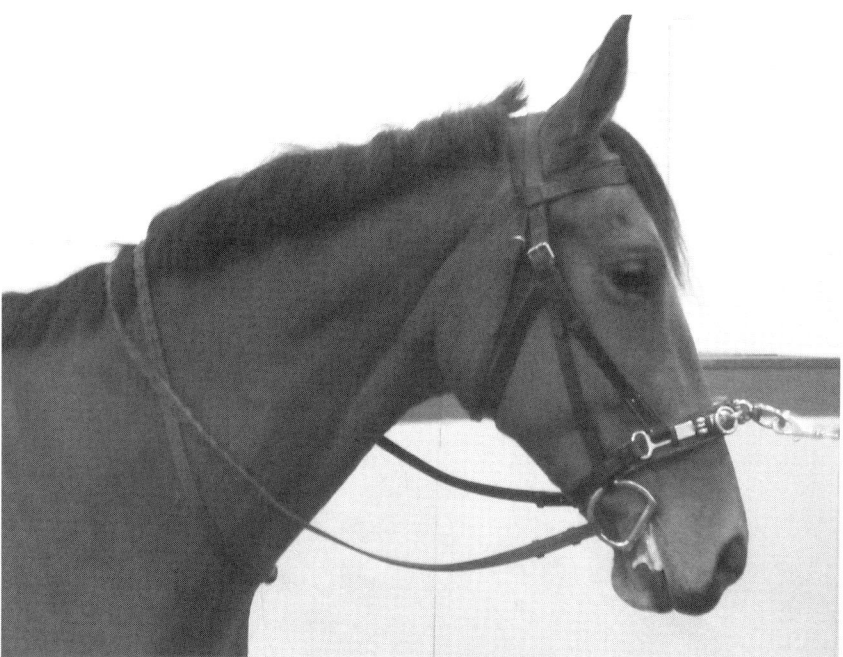
Reins looped around the horses neck for longeing with a rider.

Longe lessons are intense, and therefore must be kept short—30 minutes at the most—with frequent changes of direction and breaks for both the horse and rider. Working for too long at a stretch can result in an unintentional practice of incorrect posture and technique as the rider compensates for exhausted muscle groups. For similar reasons, it is important to keep the circle large. Small circles increase stress for both the horse and the rider. The centrifugal force that pushes the rider to the outside becomes stronger as the circle becomes smaller. A larger circle, therefore, will help the rider to maintain balance while avoiding over-stressing any particular muscle groups.

Due in part to the time constraints, the instructor is obligated to keep the longe lesson plans simple. Limiting the focus of the lesson to one narrow topic also helps to ensure that the topic is thoroughly communicated to the student, minimizes the need for repetition in later lessons, and encourages a steady rate of progress.

With simplified lessons, information presented can often be mastered the same day. Each lesson builds slightly on what came before. Skills are built in

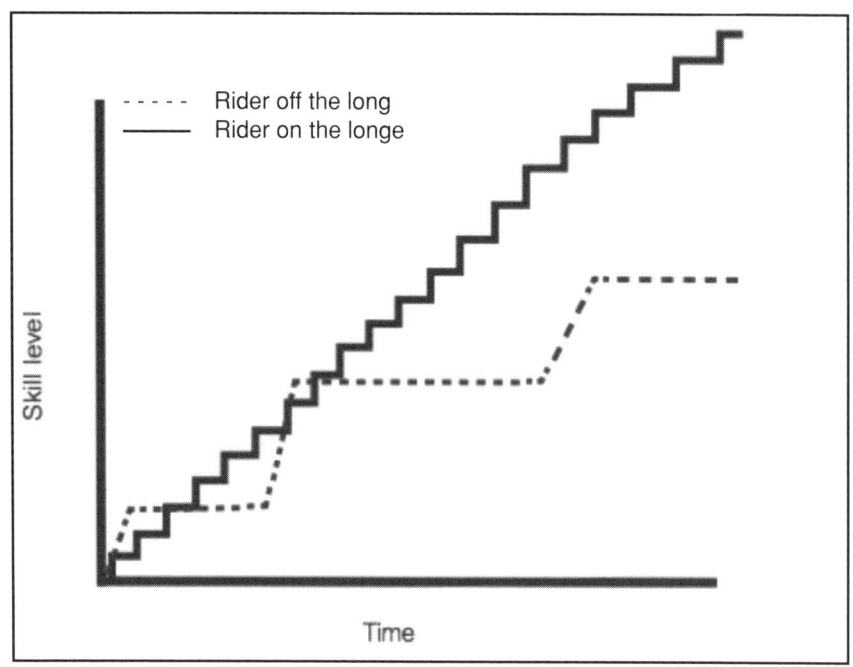

The many small steps possible in a longe lesson ultimately result in much faster progress than the large leaps and plateaus necessary for students who don't have the benefit of longe lessons.

manageably small but noticeable steps so that frustration and struggle are kept to a minimum and the joy of accomplishment is kept high. In this way, complex skills are developed bit by bit and generally are mastered more quickly overall than by the student to whom the skills were presented all at once, followed by a plateau. During these plateaus, students often struggle, frustrated by their inability to perform the skill. For example, when a student initially learns to canter without the longe, she is generally expected to learn the aids to the canter and the feel of the canter rhythm, how to sit the canter, how to control the horse in the canter, and how to bring the horse back to the trot or the walk—all in one lesson. She then spends many more lessons learning to coordinate these tasks. On the longe, these can be divided up into individual lessons. Each can be mastered individually and, due to the focused attention of both student and instructor, quickly.

## TO USE OR NOT TO USE STIRRUPS

It is often assumed that in longe lessons the student rides without stirrups. While there certainly are benefits to working without stirrups, they primarily apply to students in the later stages of the training scale (suppleness and feel) and beyond. Work without stirrups, when done too early, actually interferes with rider development rather than promoting it. It creates tension, disturbs balance, and promotes the development of incorrect muscle groups. The muscles of the upper and inner thigh are particularly over-used by insufficiently prepared riders who do not use stirrups. Far from holding the rider on the horse, pinching in this area actually pushes the rider up off the horse's back; therefore, use of these muscles is directly at odds with the development of a deep seat and must be avoided. Before work without stirrups can be beneficial, "suppleness" must be fairly well established. Therefore, correct work without stirrups will be discussed more thoroughly in Chapter 6.

## ON YOUR OWN

In order to reap the many benefits of longe lessons, you will clearly need a friend. As was mentioned earlier in the chapter, if your friend is not an experienced longe instructor, it is of greater importance that the horse be calm and straight and have a steady tempo. The most important thing for your friend to know is how to keep the horse showing these traits; i.e., the horse may not be allowed to drift in or out of the prescribed circle, and he may not sporadically speed up or slow down. If he does, then you, the rider will be distracted from your goal: to improve yourself. If you experience these distractions, be sure to let your friend know what you feel the horse doing. It will help to train her eye and to hone her skill (as long as you tell her nicely!) in detecting the very slight change in the horse's movement from the center of the circle that feels like a much bigger deal from the horse's back. And by all means, trade places occasionally. There is nothing like being longed to create a sympathetic longe instructor! If you can't find a willing friend, keep trying. In the meantime, check out Chapter 10, "Off the Longe."

# CHAPTER 2

# RELAXATION

The first step on the training scale is the same for all students, both human and equine. In the presence of fear, there will be no learning; therefore, it must be eradicated first. Beyond that, we all carry reserves of tension somewhere in our body. Many people carry tension in their shoulders. Some clench their jaws. Wherever the individual holds tension, if it is recognized, it can more effectively be released, and both riding and learning will become easier.

Lack of tension does not mean lack of muscle tone. In other words, the goal is not to make the rider resemble gelatin. This is often misunderstood. Postural muscles (also known as core muscles)—the ones that keep us sitting up straight—need to maintain their tone without tension. The goal is to remove excessive or unnecessary tension so that the rider's body is not working against itself and the rider can direct her energies toward learning.

Mental and physical tension are separate but related issues that must be dealt with differently, though they may feed off of one another. The only circumstance in which physical tension takes priority (in terms of being dealt with first) is if the student is so far out of position that she cannot possibly relax. In this case, a basic correction to the rider's position provides a large measure of relief instantly. In all other cases, mental tension (anxiety) should be dealt with first. The reasoning behind this is that much physical tension is the result of anxiety. If the anxiety is released, the muscular tension will vanish. However, trying to relieve the physical tension in the presence of mental tension will probably result in an increase in both types, because the student is being asked to do something of which she is not capable.

Mental tension reveals itself in many ways, most of which are instinctively recognizable: wide eyes, pale face, facial tension, whole-body tension, and/or rapid, shallow breaths. For such a rider, usually an inexperienced one, much tension can be released by simple conversation. Holding one's breath is a common symptom of tension, and causes tension as well, resulting in a cyclical effect. The fact is that, if a person is talking, she must be breathing! Many new riders find it reassuring to talk about the horse's actions. Why, for example, is the horse raising/lowering/turning his head? What has caught his attention? If the rider has a specific fear, discuss it (for example, being thrown). What is the likelihood of this happening? Why do horses buck? What might trigger the feared behavior? When is the last time this horse exhibited the feared behavior? (If he is a suitable lesson horse, the answer should be a reassuringly long time.) Much fear comes from lack of knowledge and understanding; therefore, anytime an instructor can increase the rider's level of understanding of her equine partner, that instructor simultaneously decreases the fear of the unknown and takes the rider one step closer to being a horseman.

Some riders are too focused on the horse. Whether this is the case can be determined by observing the rider's visual focus—she looks straight down at the horse's neck with wide eyes! This kind of rider may need a bit of distraction to bring her out of herself and back into a safer awareness of her surroundings. A question about the rider's job, school, or even the weather can gently and easily have the desired effect.

Physical tension that is not attached to mental tension is generally localized. Many people clench their jaws or hunch their shoulders in concentration. Others clench their fists or lock their wrists or elbows (a powerful argument against giving reins to beginners). Any joint can be locked due to tension. The wise instructor makes no assumptions about where tension will manifest. To release locked joints and tense muscles, gentle movements are very effective. Moving requires that muscles alternately contract and relax. For example, to bend the arm at the elbow, the biceps muscle (agonist) contracts, while the triceps (antagonist) relaxes. To extend the arm, the opposite occurs: the triceps becomes the agonist and contracts, while the biceps, as the antagonist, relaxes. All skeletal muscles come in agonist/antagonist pairs. Without relaxation, therefore, movement is impossible. When people are afraid, they sometimes freeze because both muscles of the pair are contracted simultaneously. After the fear is relieved, the muscular tension often lingers. People often don't realize that they have locked a set of muscles until they attempt movement, and then they feel the release of the antagonist muscle. Therefore, gentle movements are good, relaxing exercises.

# RELAXATION 25

Tension does not occur only in the inexperienced, however. The advanced rider on an unfamiliar horse or in an unfamiliar situation will harbor tension. So will the person who just had a bad day at the office, even though she is riding her own, familiar horse. Relaxation exercises are a great way to put outside worries aside so that the rider may focus on and enjoy her time with the horse.

(Left): Lift the thigh away from the saddle one at a time to relax the inner thigh.

(Below, Left and Right): Scissors kicks, from the hip.

## 26 Training Tree for Riders

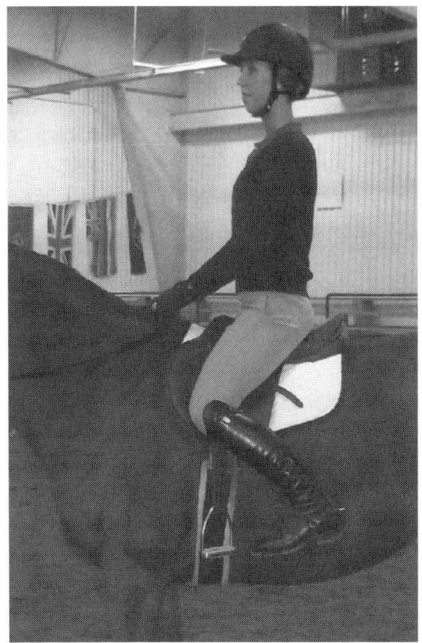 

Scissors kicks, from the knee.

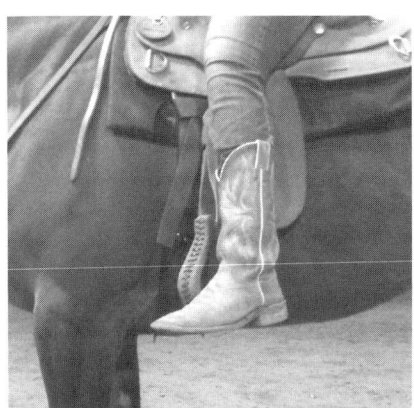 

With your feet out of the stirrups, rotate your toes in a circle.

## RELAXATION 27

(All Photos, This Page): Arm rotations—
up and back, not forward and down.

## 28  Training Tree for Riders

(Left): Tilt your head gently from side to side and from front to back.

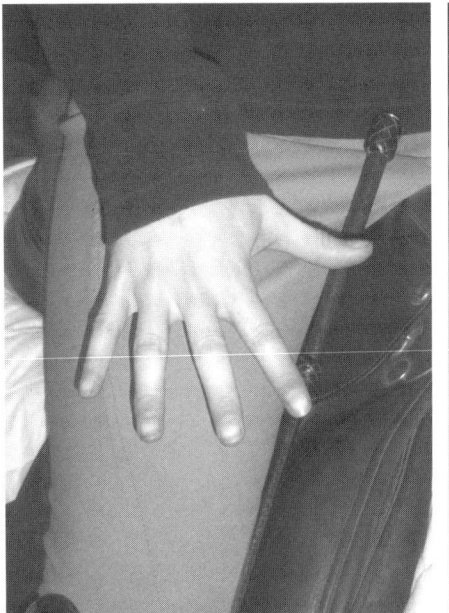 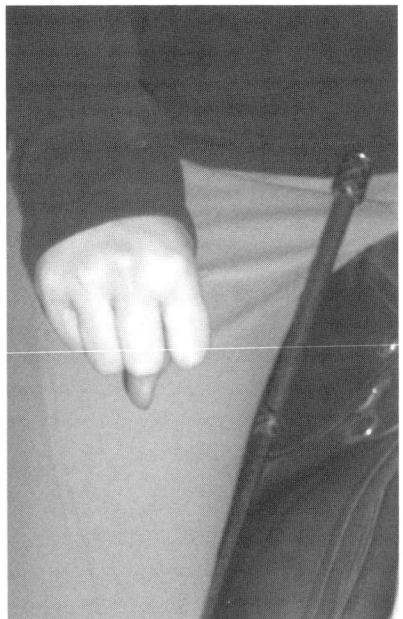

(Above): Opening and closing the fingers.

# RELAXATION

Shoulder circles.

## FOCUSED RELAXATION

When the rider is comfortable enough to close her eyes, exercises in focused relaxation can begin. It is not necessary for the student to practice this before moving on to the next step on the scale. In fact, this exercise is perhaps most useful as part of a warm-up toward a more advanced step, further on in the rider's education.

Focused relaxation consists quite simply of focusing attention on a particular body part and releasing any tension that is discovered. It is a skill that is developed through practice and a very useful one at that—not just for riding, but in any time of stress or when a person is having difficulty relaxing.

Initial practice is best done off the horse. To begin, lie down on the floor or on a firm mat (cushions and mattresses have too much give) in a neutral position, as shown in the photo at the top of the next page. The position

Neutral position.

should be symmetrical, with no overlap of body parts. The feet should be a few inches apart and parallel to one another. The knees may wobble at first, but with practice they will balance naturally over the hips and feet.

Close your eyes. Breathe. Feel your feet on the floor. Be aware of each bone against the floor. Allow the weight of your leg to spread through these bones. As you inhale, feel your breath extend all the way to your feet. As you exhale, let go of all of the tension in your feet. Take as many breaths as necessary to release all of the tension.

Follow the bones of your lower leg up to your knee, acknowledging and exhaling tension as you go. Imagine that your knees are hanging by strings from the rafters; they do not need to lean against one another for support or be held with tense muscles. Release their tension.

Continue along the thigh to the pelvis, feeling the muscles melting with relaxation as you go. Pause, and spend a moment in the pelvis. Your breath easily extends to here. Feel the bones of your pelvis against the floor, with your weight equally supported on both sides.

As you continue up the torso, feel your rib cage as it expands in all directions with every breath: side to side, front to back. Feel your shoulder blades fall against the floor. Follow the bones of your arm slowly out to your fingertips. Notice any tension along the way, and let it go with the next breath.

When you are ready, follow your vertebrae up the neck. Let go with the muscles of the neck. Allow the floor to support the head. And then spend a few moments at your head. Relax your scalp, and forehead, Relax your jaw and mouth. Relax your cheeks and lips. Relax your eyes. Let them rest in their sockets.

Enjoy the relaxation. Slowly, when you are ready, open your eyes. Look softly on the world. Gently sit up, and then stand, with your weight balanced on both feet.

Now stretch your spine tall, as if you were a marionette being pulled up by a string on top of your head. Tip just your chin down, to flex the first vertebrae—the atlas. Feel the muscles stretch along the back of your neck. Then con-

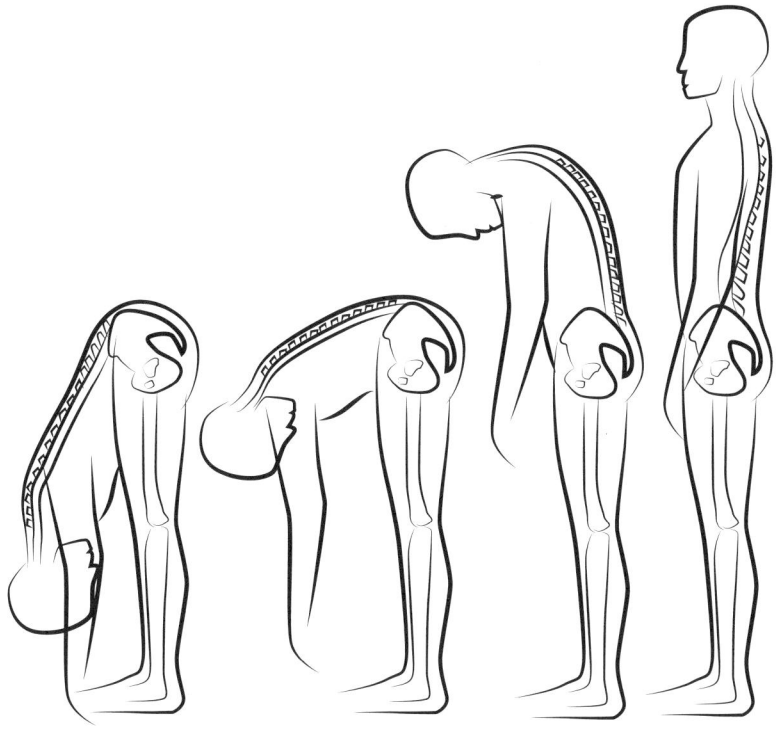

Stacking vertebrae: start with your whole upper body completely limp. The first step to restacking the vertebrae is to tilt the pelvis. Then, continue to place more vertebrae back in place, while still allowing the upper vertebrae to hang, until… Voila! Your back is straighter than ever!

tinue flexing vertebrae, as few as possible at a time: first those in the neck, then in the thorax and the abdomen, until your upper body hangs from your hips.

Now slowly, one vertebra at a time and starting at the bottom, stack them back up again. First tilt only the pelvis back and allow the rest of the back to round. Then gradually bring the vertebrae of the lower back into line while letting the upper back hang round. Now, one by one, lift the thoracic vertebrae with the ribs, then the cervical vertebrae of the neck, until the skull is lifted to the top as if pulled by a string from the ceiling.

If you are like most people, your rib cage is now farther in front of you than normal. Although the newness of it seems strange, it is biologically more correct than slouching. Your internal organs can work more efficiently. Getting into the habit of carrying yourself this way is a wonderful gift to yourself. Don't try to hold the position, though, as that will create tension; just restack your vertebrae as needed. The more you practice, the sooner it will become habit.

Along with rounding the back, many people hunch their shoulders forward. To release and open the shoulders, do several arm circles, one arm at a time, slowly: up, back, and around. With the help of these exercises, you should be standing up straight in almost no time, and your body, not to mention your horse, will love you for it!

Focused relaxation done mounted is a bit more difficult because of the muscular tone required to sit up and maintain balance. It is nevertheless a worthwhile exercise because it teaches the rider kinesthetic awareness, which will be very important in the development of "Feel" and for noticing and releasing tension. It can be practiced at a halt or later at a walk.

Begin focused relaxation with the pelvis when mounted. Ask that the rider feel weight equally in both seat bones and the pubic bone. If this is the case, the pelvis will be upright. If the rider is uncertain, rocking the pelvis forward and backward on the seat bones can be useful to differentiate straight from tipped in either direction. Once the meaning of "straight" is recognized, have the rider relax and allow her pelvis to move along with the horse's back (if walking). Ask her to drop the stirrups, allowing her legs to hang naturally, but not exaggeratedly, or the hips will again be pulled askew.

Verbally guide the rider's awareness down the leg, asking simply that she be aware of each segment in turn, and, if tension is discovered, that it be released. When finished, assist the rider in returning her feet to the stirrups. If she is allowed to struggle with them, tension will surely return. Draw her attention to the fact that only a very slight change in leg position should be required by the stirrups. The toe will need to flex upward; the knee will lift as the toe enters the stirrup but then should settle right back. Most riders want to push their feet forward into the stirrup, but no change in the rider's vertical alignment should take place.

Continue the relaxation process up through the abdomen and beyond, in much the same way as was done unmounted. Have the rider feel the deep breathing, allowing lungs to expand in every direction—down to the pelvis, from side to side, and from front to back. The breastbone should be lifted so that the shoulder blades fall back and the arms hang free. The bones of the arm are then followed slowly out to the fingertips; the rider should notice any tension along the way and let it go with the next breath.

When the rider is ready, the vertebrae are followed up the neck, and the muscles of the neck are let go. The head is balanced over the neck.

A few moments are then spent at the head. The scalp, forehead, jaw, and mouth are relaxed. The cheeks and lips are relaxed. The eyes are relaxed. They should rest in their sockets.

Ending with "stacking the vertebrae" may not be possible due to the limited range for leaning forward, but arm circles can be included.

When you are finished, talk with your rider. If she is aware of a location in her body that still feels tense, you may need to help her adjust her position to allow its release. Throughout the ride, if you see that tension creeps in, mention it to the rider, help her to become more aware, and help her to release the tension. The more this exercise is practiced, both on and off the horse, the more effective it becomes.

## POSTURE AND RELAXATION

Posture is important to relaxation. The human body is meant to be supported by bones and postural muscles. When posture is not correct, as is the case with most of us, the job of maintaining posture falls to muscles that are not intended or suited to the purpose. These muscles will ache and even spasm when they are particularly stressed, resulting in backaches, neck pain, and headaches. When these overburdened muscles are called upon to do the job for which they were intended as well, they may lack the expected strength and range of motion.

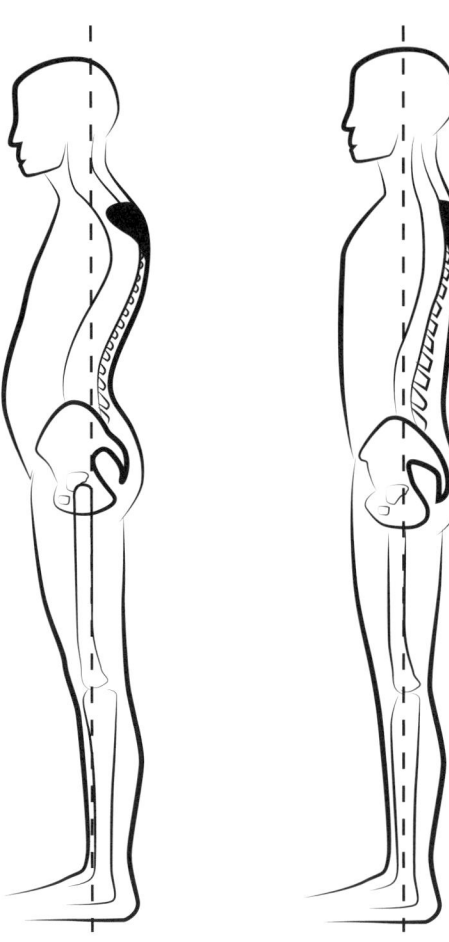

A spine in correct alignment possesses natural, gentle curves. In incorrect alignment, some of these may be exaggerated, or lost. Notice that when the back is aligned correctly, the shoulder blades are free to drop to their lowest position, but if the back is slouched, the shoulder blades lay against the ribcage which interferes with their freedom of movement.

Correct posture allows the body to work efficiently, and in harmony, with minimum tension. In order to ride well, all of the rider's bones and muscles must be freed from unnecessary burdens so that they can do the job for which they were intended. This is the goal of relaxation.

When postural muscles are called upon to perform their tasks after years of disuse, the unfamiliar sensation and the resultant change in balance may result in some stiffness. The student may need extra help relaxing within the framework of posture. Correct posture does not involve tension. If the student cannot release tension and maintain posture, then she is not achieving correct posture in the first place. The rider may, for example, be pulling the shoulders back rather than lifting the sternum (breastbone) forward and upward until the shoulders fall back of their own accord. Spotting the difference requires a careful eye and clear communication from instructor to student and student to instructor. It is very well worth the effort.

## ON YOUR OWN

Before greeting your horse, spend a few minutes in a quiet place. Breathe deeply into your abdomen. Let go of your day's tensions. Clear your mind. Do not rush. When you are ready, bring your attention back around to the present activity and to your horse.

Most horses easily accept the movements involved in performing the relaxation exercises described in this chapter, so you should have no trouble doing them. Start your ride with these exercises as your horse warms up in a walk, and repeat them as needed. Don't be afraid to stop right in the middle of something else that you are working on to verify, confirm, or regain relaxation. Chances are, the "something else" will come much more easily once you have done so. Horses do not have a sixth sense for fear, as is often believed, but tension does interfere with communication via body language. If you are struggling, and your horse doesn't seem to want to cooperate, you might just be trying so hard that your tension is interfering with your aids or blocking your horse in his attempts to comply. Do your relaxation exercises, breathe deeply, and then carefully ask again. That is often all that is needed to get the response that you seek.

## MOVING ON

Some people seem to have been born relaxed, while for others relaxation requires quite a bit of practice and attention. Ideally, the rider should be completely free of tension at all times. Realistically, relaxation is, in part, a function of exposure and familiarity. That is, the more time the student spends on the horse's back, the more she will feel at ease there. This may take several lessons to develop, but that is not to say that relaxation must necessarily be the sole focus of each lesson during this time.

Each lesson should begin with relaxation exercises. When the student has released all fear and outside concerns and stresses, then she is mentally relaxed enough to focus on what she is experiencing at the moment, and on learning. The student must then relax enough physically to not develop sore muscles (which she will not realize until later, after the tension has been released) or be irritating to or interfere with the horse.

When these basic conditions of mental and physical relaxation have been met, then relaxation may not need to be the primary focus any longer. Balance exercises may commence. As the student develops competence at each successive step on the tree, relaxation will be enhanced because confidence will grow, and therefore anxiety will lessen. If the opposite trend is noted, it is a clear sign that the student is being pushed along too quickly and is feeling overwhelmed. It is also important to note that the more advanced the rider, the greater the level of relaxation required, both mental and physical, so as not to interfere with the fine communication that must exist, or be developing, between the horse and rider. Several authors have written about achieving a meditative level of relaxation to enhance the rider's, and therefore the horse's, performance, particularly at advanced levels. Achieving relaxation remains an indispensable part of the daily routine.

# CHAPTER 3

# BALANCE

Balance is instinctive. If a rider is not able to balance automatically, for example, due to neurological problems or an inner ear infection, she must not ride. It would be terribly unsafe. On the other hand, if our instinct to balance were flawless, no one would ever fall! Balancing in a new situation, such as on a boat or a horse, requires some practice but will become second nature with practice.

## VERTICAL BALANCE

New riders, of course, often associate sitting on a horse with sitting on a chair. In fact, sitting in a chair is only balanced as long as the person and the chair remain still. A person must shift her weight significantly forward (over the feet) before arising. Imagine what would befall the chair sitter if the chair were suddenly to vanish! Horses tend not to remain still (which is entirely the point of riding, right?). In fact, they occasionally seem to vanish suddenly from beneath our seat. Therefore, changing this preconception is key to achieving a dynamic balance—one that can change to accommodate the horse's movements without deteriorating.

With the rider in proper vertical alignment, the center of mass is directly above the heel, and the weight should pass through the seat, down to the heels. This position is similar to that required of most athletes and martial artists because it allows a dynamic balance. For riding, we generally prefer an upright torso; therefore, correct posture is easily recognized by the fact that we could draw a straight, vertical line from the rider's ear, through her shoulder and hip, and ending in her heel (not behind her heel). Even if the student found this alignment on her own or with the instructor's help, as part of the relaxation phase, she will likely need further encouragement to really allow her weight, and center of gravity, to drop lower. Visualization exercises can be useful, such as one from Sally Swift's Centered Riding, wherein the rider is asked to imagine that her chest is packed with wet sand. As the sand dries, it trickles to her feet, transferring its weight, and therefore the rider's center of gravity, lower.

Once the rider's weight is distributed down the leg and through relaxed ankles, the rider can be encouraged to keep it there while moving the upper body. Reaching forward and back with each arm, or with both together, is a very good exercise as long as balance is maintained. If the student leans on the horse's neck in an attempt to reach further forward, for example, her center of gravity will no longer be low, and if the horse lowers his head, the rider could easily somersault off.

(Left) Various arm positions challenge the rider's balance as well as adding variety to otherwise familiar exercises. Don't underestimate the effect of changing the arm position on the overall balance of the rider. Arms are 5 to 6 percent of your body weight each—a significant amount to balance.

(Right) Hands on the hips.

**BALANCE** 39

Hands on the shoulders.

Helicopters.

## 40   *Training Tree for Riders*

Hands behind the back.

Arms out in front.

Hands on the head.

**BALANCE** 41

One hand over the head.

Positions can be put together in any combination.

Two-point position is an excellent exercise for balance. It is an easy position to maintain as long as vertical alignment is correct. Any deviation from verticality will very quickly be revealed: if the leg is too far forward, the rider will tend to fall back into the saddle; if the leg is too far back, the rider will tend to fall forward onto the horse's neck. For this reason, it is an exercise worth doing (and teaching) even if the rider never intends to jump. Two-point position is achieved by the rider rocking her weight forward off the seat and onto her thigh. Her seat should be slightly above the saddle and her hands stretched forward about one-third to one-half of the way up the horse's neck. The rider's knees remain bent so that her seat stays close to the saddle seat while the hips fold, allowing the back to remain flat. This will bring the shoulders in front of the vertical line through the heel and center of gravity, and the hips behind it, although the center of gravity itself, located just behind the belly button, will remain over the heels. For more on this, and other exercises, see "On Your Own" at the end of this chapter.

Two-point position.

# BALANCE 43

Two-point position.

A distressingly high percentage of riders ride in a slight chair seat while imagining themselves correct. This imbalance leaves the rider perpetually behind the motion, making her more difficult for the horse to carry. As a result, her performance will probably suffer. It slows reaction time on the rider's behalf and requires the use of more muscular tension to maintain position, which interferes with relaxation and ultimately renders the rider more likely to perform an "unexpected dismount."

## 44  *Training Tree for Riders*

Nearly correct alignment—the rider is leaning forward slightly.

A chair seat spoils an otherwise lovely position.

Again, it must be stressed that, without a properly fitting saddle, a correct seat will be impossible. Be aware, too, of saddles that have an incorrect design; for example, with stirrup bars set too far forward. These saddles do not allow a balanced position even when the size is appropriate to both horse and rider.

Assuming saddle design and fit are correct, correcting the chair seat begins with bringing the rider's pelvis forward. Although it is frequently heard, no amount of "bring your leg back" will be effective until the seat is positioned correctly over the stirrups. A very effective tool to help the rider develop the habit of sitting toward the front of the saddle is to tie a polo wrap around the cantle with the knot on top. Once the rider sits correctly in the saddle, the legs may well take care of themselves. If the legs do need to come back, they almost always need to come back from the hip joint. Only rarely is correction as simple as bending the knee to bring the lower leg back.

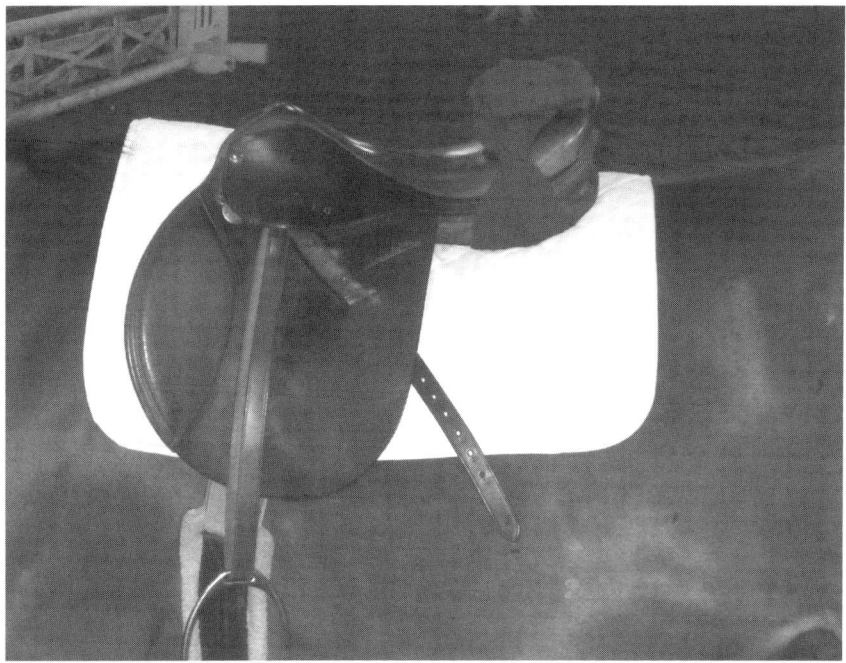

A polo wrap tied around the cantle is one way to encourage the rider to sit forward over her feet.

46  *Training Tree for Riders*

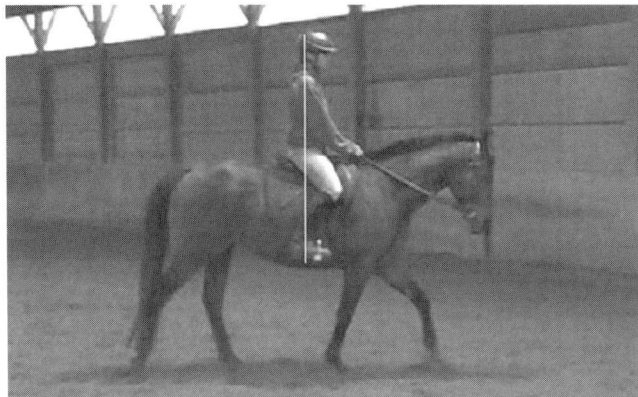

Correct alignment in a walk.

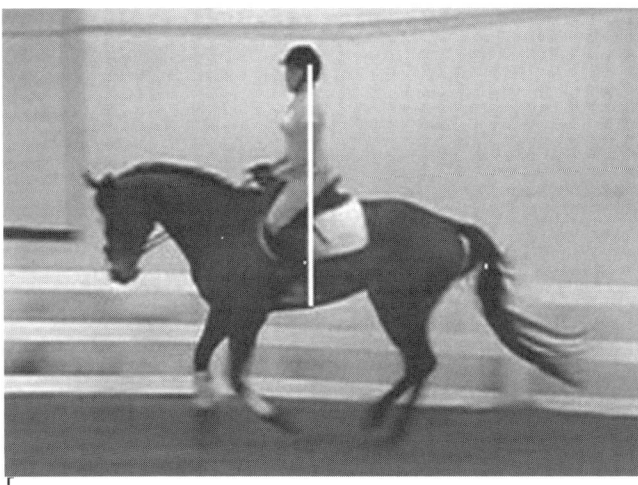

Correct alignment in a canter.

## LATERAL BALANCE

In addition to vertical alignment, riders must have correct lateral balance. Most people lack symmetry in their muscular development. Our left- or right-handedness affects our entire body. In riding, this often presents as sitting to one side. The stronger leg pulls the rider toward it and then continues to support a majority of the rider's weight. The sooner the rider is made aware of any asymmetries, the sooner she can begin to develop the weaker leg by shifting her weight toward it and forcing the weak leg to carry its share of weight, and the sooner she can begin to develop a sense of relative straightness.

# BALANCE 47

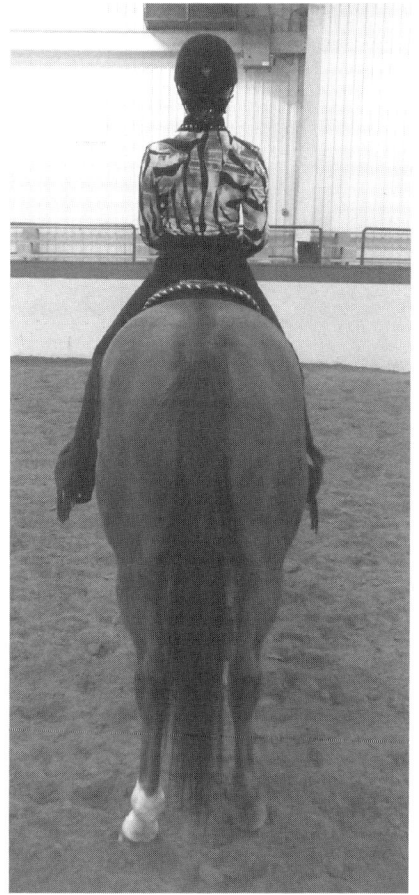 

The straight rider.      The crooked rider.

The term "relative straightness" is important here, for in riding on a circle, the horse is not straight (geometrically speaking); therefore, the rider should not be symmetrical. "The rider's shoulders should mirror the horse's shoulders, and the rider's hips should mirror the horse's hips" is an often-quoted truism. Therefore, it is during this stage that the rider should begin to be encouraged to ride a "spiral seat," with the outside leg back, the inside hip relatively forward, and the shoulders turned gently in the direction of travel. In this position, the rider mirrors the horse's bend.

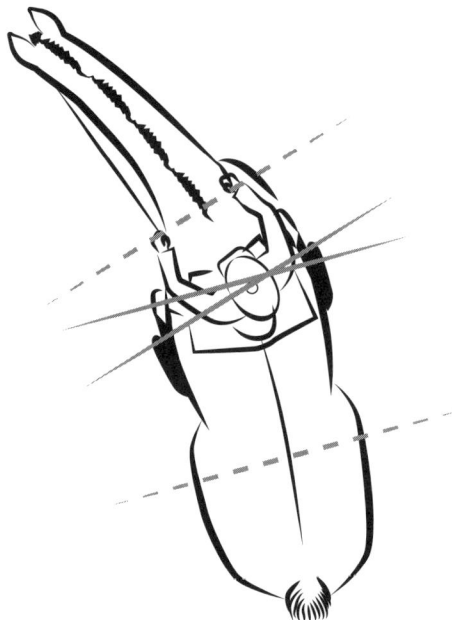

Compare the angle of the rider's shoulders to the horse's shoulders, and the angle of the rider's hips to the horse's hips.

The rider's hips should be parallel to the horse's hips, and the rider's shoulders should be parallel to the horse's shoulders to allow the greatest ease of performance

Lateral balance can be a little tricky on the longe. Having students first learn to ride on the longe has much to recommend it and very few drawbacks. One potential drawback is the possibility of the rider's balance shifting to the outside of the circle due to centrifugal force. This is one of the reasons why frequent changes of direction and breaks to a walk are necessary. It will also help if the rider is reminded to step more deeply into the inside stirrup and to slide her hips just slightly toward the inside of the circle, or to "sit over the inside stirrup," as should always be done when riding a bending line or a movement with bend.

It is a good idea to occasionally have an assistant longe the student so that you, the instructor, may teach from the outside of the circle. From this vantage point, in addition to viewing your rider from the side, you will be able to observe as she rides toward and away from you—ideal for spotting lateral asymmetries. Encourage the rider to develop an awareness of such aspects of her position as having both seat bones in the saddle, with equal weight on each one, and having equal contact between each thigh and the saddle. Listen carefully as the rider describes one-sided difficulties, and watch for her to tire more easily in one direction than the other. The horse can also offer important clues about a rider's asymmetries as he is strongly affected by the rider's balance or lack thereof. Look for clues such as differing quality of gaits, movement, or transitions in one direction as compared to the other.

In a nutshell, in any way in which the rider's position does not feel symmetrical, the asymmetry should reverse with the direction. For example, it is understandable that the inside leg may tire more easily because it carries more weight. If the left leg tires more easily regardless of direction, then lateral balance probably needs to be addressed.

## ON YOUR OWN

The subtleties of balance are demons for many riders. The difficulty lies in the fact that there are many different balances, or ways of balancing. If you have ridden for any length of time, you have no doubt developed your own form of balance. A chair seat, for example, is balanced similarly to a three-legged stool—a very stable design as long as you are on a flat, stable surface. I have yet to meet a flat, stable horse! A rider should be balanced over her feet with the knees slightly bent, in a similar position to most other athletes, in order to be able to fluidly adjust to the actions of her teammate, the horse (something a stool cannot do). Because you have already found a certain balance, any change will initially feel unbalanced, even if it is a change for the better. Improving your balance, therefore, requires checking many times per ride for verification and feedback.

To check your lateral balance—that is, whether you are sitting in the center of the saddle—include marching steps in your warm-up. By raising each leg in turn so that the knee comes up to or above the pommel of your saddle, you are taking away the ability of your legs to hide the crookedness of your seat. If you find that you do need to adjust your seat to one side in order to complete the exercise, then you should repeat this at frequent intervals during each ride because you are likely to slide off center again. This exercise can be performed at any gait for added challenge!

Marching steps will let you know if you are sitting in the middle of the saddle.

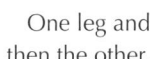

One leg and then the other.

## BALANCE 51

Two very effective exercises for checking vertical alignment are two-point position and posting at a halt or a walk. Both are very easy exercises when done correctly and become much more difficult when the rider's position is not balanced. If leg position is correct, it is nearly effortless for the rider to push herself up out of the saddle and to support herself there. If the leg is too far forward, the rider will struggle to rise from the saddle and will have to fight constantly against gravity pulling her backward again. Legs too far back will cause the rider to tip forward.

A rider with the leg too far back will tend to tip forward.

A rider with the leg too far forward will tend to fall back into the saddle.

Two-point position is achieved by rocking your weight forward off your seat and onto your thigh. The seat should be slightly above the saddle, and your hands should be stretched forward about one-third to one-half of the way up the horse's neck. Keep your knees bent so that your seat stays close to the saddle seat, and fold slightly at the hips, keeping your back flat.

Posting is essentially standing up and sitting down in the rhythm of the horse's movement, although the rider actually achieves the movement by shifting her weight from the seat bones forward to the mid-thigh while raising her seat out of the saddle. It makes riding the trot much easier, because you miss half of the bumps, but the trot also provides the initial lift to boost you up and out of the saddle. At a walk or a halt, you—the rider—bear sole responsibility for lifting yourself out of the saddle, and therein lies the challenge! As with two-point, it will be easy if you are in balance. If it is difficult, or becomes difficult after several repetitions, stop and adjust your position. You should feel as though you are pushing yourself up from the lower leg and heel. If you feel the strain in the front of the thigh, your foot is too far forward. Finally, be sure that you lower yourself back into the saddle in a controlled fashion, and do not just collapse your weight onto your horse's back. If you are not sure whether what you are feeling is correct, try moving your leg either forward or backward and try posting again. Whichever position feels easiest is the closest to correct.

When you can do both of these exercises with ease consistently, you can increase the challenge in a trot. Two-point in the trot will have the added benefit of lowering your center of gravity and develop the flexibility of your knees and ankles, in addition to testing your balance. Posting in a trot is relatively easy, as was discussed, unless you get creative! Instead of one beat up and one beat down, try two beats up and one beat down, or some other variation. As with posting in a walk, it's easy if your alignment is correct.

# CHAPTER 4

# RHYTHM

The first two steps, relaxation and balance, can be introduced at a halt. Rhythm is the first step that requires movement. The previous two steps will be somewhat disrupted with the introduction of movement, and again each time the rhythm of the movement changes, and will need to be reestablished. The student frequently accomplishes this on her own, but instructors must be ready to spend some more time on relaxation, balance, or both, if needed, with the addition of each new rhythm.

When the rider is ready, she can be helped to feel the rhythm of the horse's movement in several ways:

1. By being mounted on a horse with a clear and steady rhythm.
2. By having an instructor who can describe the gait quantitatively, in terms of the number of beats, the sequence of footfalls, and the suspension, or lack thereof.
3. By having an instructor who can describe the gait qualitatively: faster, slower, bouncy, choppy, rocking, or like a boat on the water. The more vividly the instructor can describe a new gait, the more quickly the rider will be able to find the rhythm amidst the jostling.

## THE WALK

In the walk, the horse's back shifts rhythmically toward the left hind leg, then the left front, then the right hind, and finally the right front, before starting over again. The gentle rocking reminds us of the movement of a small boat on gentle waves. The "following" movements of the rider are surprisingly similar to those of walking on our own two feet (which is why therapeutic riding is effective for those who have difficulty walking). Riders only need to stretch tall and allow the hips to be carried.

## 54  Training Tree for Riders

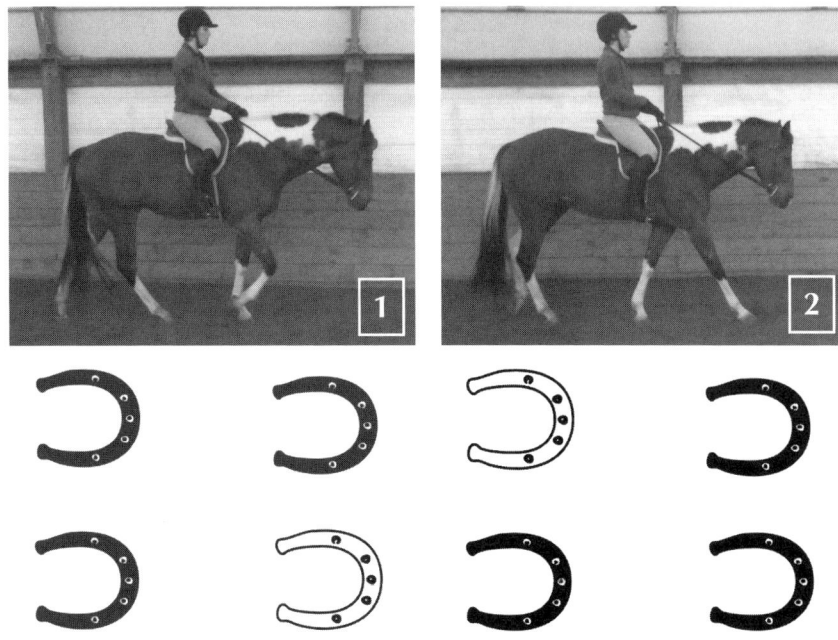

**Above and Next Page:**

In the walk, as the horse puts his foot down to push against the ground, the ground (in effect) pushes back. This "push" travels up the horse's leg to his shoulder or hip (depending on whether it is a front or back leg). The shoulder or hip, in turn, pushes on the rider. When the horse is in motion, the push won't be even.

Imagine that the horse is divided into quarters: left shoulder, right shoulder, left hip, and right hip, along with their corresponding legs. The horse's weight is supported by the legs that are on the ground. As the horse lifts a leg to take a step, that leg stops pushing at the ground, the ground stops pushing on it, and the leg/shoulder/hip stops pushing on the rider. Now imagine for a moment what would happen if one of your four chair legs stopped pushing (maybe it broke).

What would happen? You would tip toward it. That is what happens when the horse takes a step. Therefore, as the horse steps left front, then right hind, then right front, then left hind, the rider tips toward the left front, then right hind, then right front, then left hind. It is only a slight tip and most riders quickly learn to ignore it. A better alternative to ignoring it is to consciously recognize how the horse's body moves so that you can use your awareness (See Chapters 7 and 8).

# RHYTHM 55

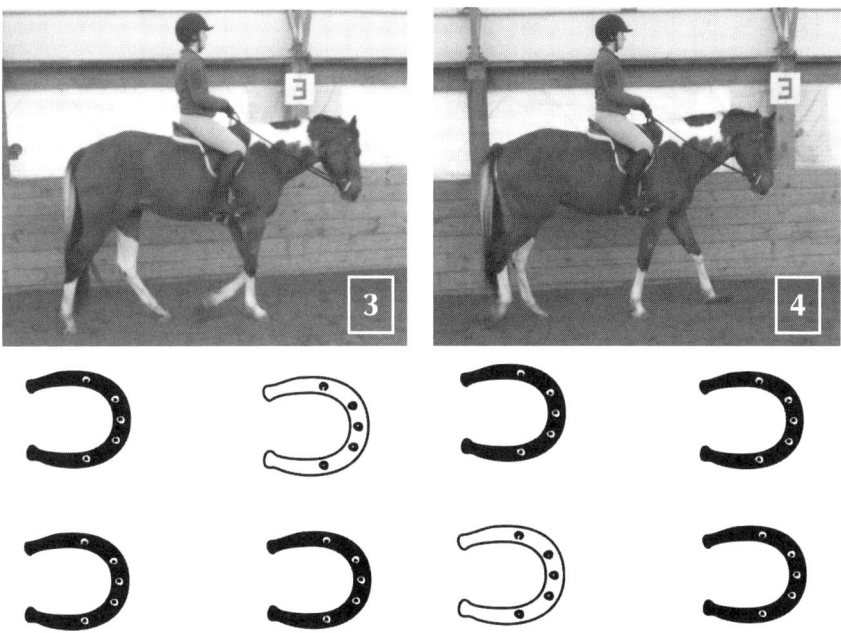

As soon as the rider feels the walk rhythm, and is relaxed and balanced in that rhythm, she can be encouraged to use her legs very gently in the rhythm of the horse's movements. As the horse's rib cage swings from side to side, the rider's legs push alternately, encouraging that rhythmic swing. As the ribs swing to the right, the rider's left leg squeezes, and as the ribs swing to the left, the rider's right leg squeezes. It's so gentle that I often describe it as "breathing in and out with the horse's sides," although it can become stronger with a horse who is having difficulty maintaining a desirable tempo.

This benefits the rider in many ways. It assists the horse in maintaining a consistent tempo, stride length, and energy level in the walk, all of which make for an easier ride. It encourages an awareness of less obvious differences between horses and within the same horse. It keeps the rider's legs always in contact with the horse's sides, ready to aid. It shifts the rider's focus from eyes and hands to legs and seat. It encourages an awareness of every step, but an awareness that can quickly become subconscious so that the rider's attention can be focused primarily on the instructor and the lesson at hand.

Horses appreciate the continuous communication from the rider, too. Nervous horses find reassurance in the rhythm so that they can relax, while sluggish horses find energy. Some may warn that horses will become dull to the aids if the rider's legs don't remain still; however, since this level of activity follows the horse's movement, it feels more still to the horse than if the rider's legs were rigid. I have never found a horse to be less responsive after having been ridden this way.

With rhythm, relaxation, and balance established in the walk, the rider can progress in two directions: either further up the scale in the walk, or mastering a new rhythm (the trot), ideally working on each for a few minutes and alternating. Changes in activity keep lessons interesting and keep the rider's muscles from becoming overly tired.

## TROT OR JOG

In the trot, the horse springs from one diagonal pair of legs (right front and left hind) and is airborne briefly before alighting on the opposite diagonal pair (left front and right hind), then he springs back again. These two moments of

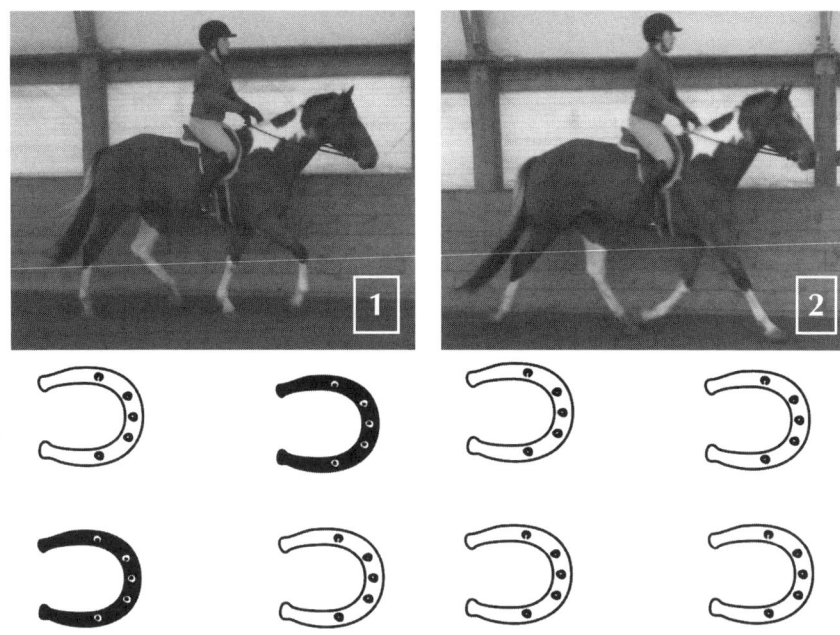

# RHYTHM 57

suspension during every stride can make for a jostling ride. Most riders new to the trot get sprung themselves from the saddle as the horse pushes off, then they land uncomfortably as the horse rises with the next step. To avoid this, riders should try posting in a walk and continue posting as the horse transitions to a trot. Soon they will be able to transition to the trot and then begin posting. Once the trot rhythm is second nature, the rider can begin sitting for short periods. See Chapter 6, "Suppleness," for more on the sitting trot.

Many believe in teaching the rider initially in a sitting trot. I believe that this practice amounts to little more than punishment for both the horse and the rider. While there is some truth to the argument that this was the method preferred by the classical schools to accustom their students to the trot rhythm

**Opposite Page and Below:**
In the trot, there is suspension. That means the horse is airborne, with no feet on the ground at some point in the stride. In fact, in the trot there are two times within each stride when the horse is airborne. This accounts for the bounciness felt by riders in the trot. Notice that the rider in the illustrations is posting, so she is only fully seated in the saddle for one of the four phases of the gait, freeing her from the jostling inherent in this gait.

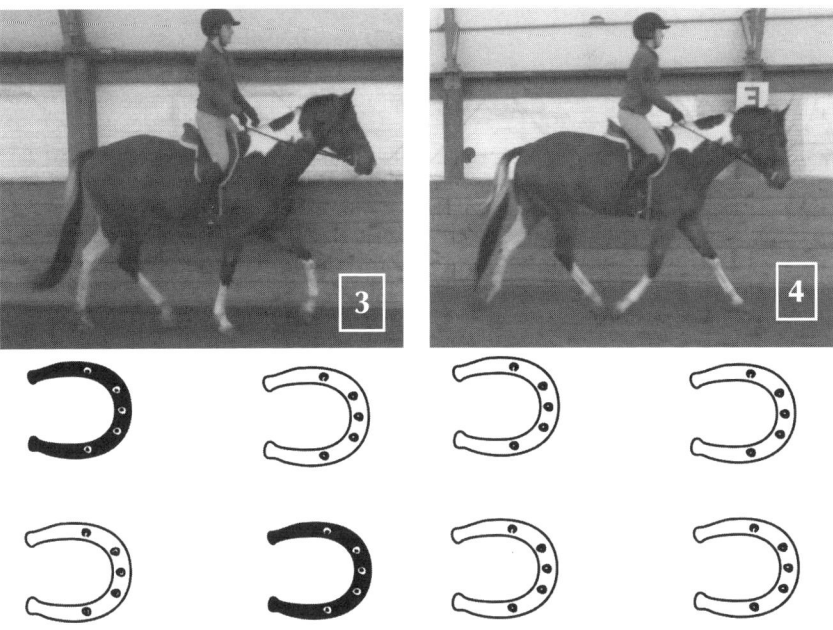

## 58  Training Tree for Riders

and develop a deep seat, it is also true that their lesson horses are/were very highly trained. The collected trot of a highly trained dressage horse bears little resemblance to the trot of a typical lesson horse. Unless your lesson horses are trained to this degree, I recommend that the posting trot be taught first. The sitting trot will be explored in Chapter 6, "Suppleness."

In the walk, the rider uses her legs alternately to reinforce a steady tempo in the horse's gait. In the trot, the rider's post has a similar effect of reinforcing the one–two rhythm of the trot. If the rider's mount needs additional support for his tempo, a squeeze of both legs in the "down" or sitting portion of the post is effective. As with the walk, the same action will have an energizing effect on a slow horse and a settling effect on an energetic horse.

## CANTER OR LOPE

In the canter, the horse rocks from the outside hind leg across the inside hind and outside fore diagonal pair to the inside front leg before lifting into a moment of suspension with all four feet off the ground. The deepest part of the

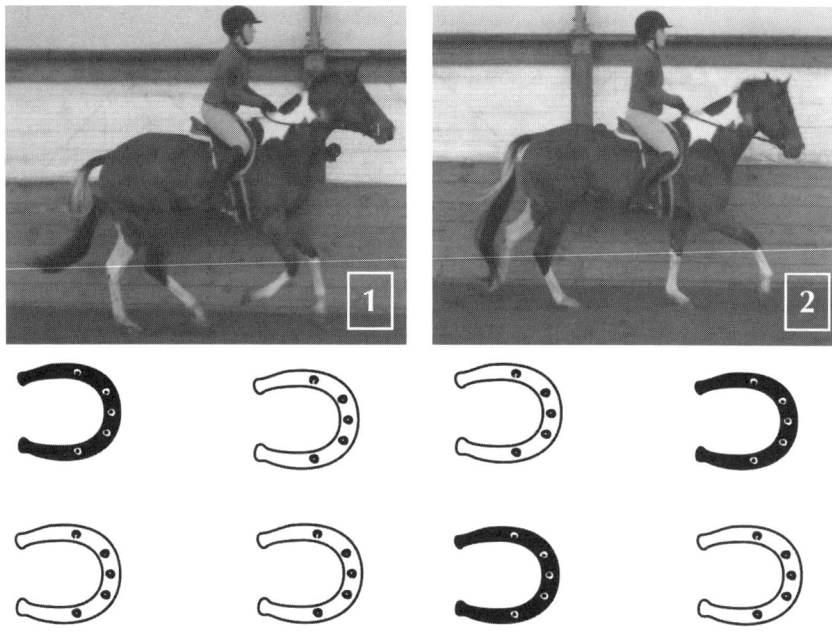

# RHYTHM 59

saddle rocks from back to front (and, to a lesser extent, from outside to inside) along with the horse's back. In order for the rider to sit in the deepest part of the saddle, her seat may have to slide from the back to the front of the saddle with each stride. As suppleness develops (Chapter 6), the degree of movement will become smaller until it is just a tilt back and forth of the hip.

Significant muscular development (see "Fitness," Chapter 5), and some suppleness (Chapter 6) are best established in the walk and trot before the rider begins to canter. In this gait, the student must follow the movement of the horse's back as he rocks from back to front as well as from side to side. With

**Opposite Page and Below:**
Like the trot, the canter has suspension, but in canter there is only one moment in the stride when the horse is airborne. The horse lands with one hind leg, rocks forward onto the two legs that constitute the diagonal pair, then rocks further forward onto the remaining front leg, and finally is airborne. Notice that the lowest part of the horse's back is over the grounded legs. The rider is seated in the lowest part of the saddle and the position of her seat in the saddle shifts forward slightly from the beginning to the end of the stride. Although her body remains very nearly vertical throughout the stride, her hip/thigh angle is changing as the horse rocks beneath her.

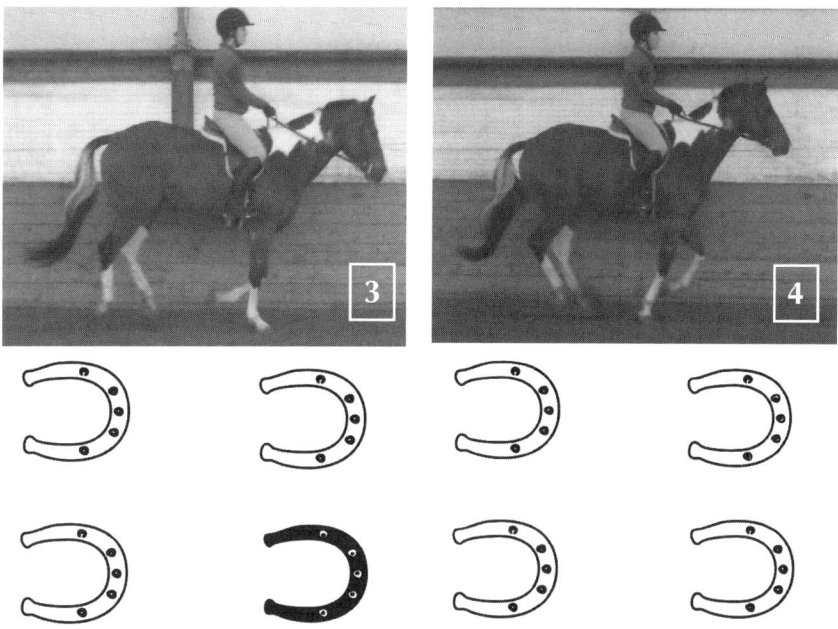

sufficient, thorough preparation in the walk and trot, it is easily assimilated by the student. Remember the principles of relative straightness (see pages 47–48) and notice that, in the canter, the position of the horse's shoulders changes. The horse's inside shoulder leads; therefore, instead of the rider turning her shoulders into the direction of travel, she should turn them slightly away. This is the reason for the common advice to look to the outside in the canter.

Some riders develop the habit of pumping their shoulders at the canter. This feels secure to the rider because her seat remains still—no bouncing! However, it is awkward for the horse, who must accommodate the rider's shifting weight and balance. It also prevents the rider from using her weight as an effective aid later on. In order to follow the horse's rocking movement in the canter, some part of the rider's body must also rock. The pumping rider incorrectly keeps her hips still and rocks the shoulders forward and backward.

An unmounted exercise to correct this has the rider place both hands on a fence rail in front of her. This will help the rider to keep her shoulders still. Now she can practice the back-and-forth movement of the hips. In order to make this change, the center of movement will have to change from the shoulder to the hip (including the knee to the waist), and the center of stability must move from the hip to the shoulder. Once the rider has grasped this on the ground, she is ready to begin to reproduce the same feeling on the cantering horse.

An unmounted exercise to assist the rider in stabilizing the shoulders.

## THE TRAINING BUSH?

This is where the non-linearity of the system becomes particularly apparent. From this point, the rider may be at a different point on the training scale in each gait for some time. The rider's progress at each step may be influenced now, not just by the previous steps along the scale, but by lateral steps as well. For example, the development of suppleness in the trot will be influenced strongly by suppleness exercises done in the walk, although they might not be worked on simultaneously.

Additionally, a step of the scale in a faster gait may benefit from the student's efforts in a more advanced step of a slower gait. For example, a student learning to ride the canter rhythm will benefit from work done previously on building muscle and suppleness in the walk and trot. Within each gait, progress along the scale remains linear. An additional diagram of how different steps are often developed simultaneously is presented in Appendix 2.

Rhythm is a step in which experienced riders benefit. Feeling and accommodating the rhythm of any gait is like riding a bicycle in that, once you learn it, you never really forget how to do it. Therefore, this step can be bypassed for the student who uses the training tree as her warm-up. On the other hand, some gaits are less similar than they may seem on the surface. For example, an experienced Western rider will need help adjusting to the forward gaits of an English-trained horse and vice versa. Although the rhythm of the jog and the trot are both two beats, the stride length and impulsion are very different.

## ON YOUR OWN

Learning rhythms on your own is not much different than learning with the help of an instructor once you have read and assimilated the information in this chapter. The biggest difference is that you may not have help getting the horse into the new rhythm. A horse that is not very responsive to the aids often tempts the rider out of position when asking for the transition to the new gait. The horse then spurts forward in the new rhythm with a faster tempo, and the rider's position completely falls apart, leaving no real chance for the new rhythm to be learned.

It would seem that the best way to avoid this is to use a horse that is highly responsive, but sensitive, responsive horses are often not forgiving when the rider makes a mistake. So what to do? There are several things. You can carry a whip; a gentle tap is far more effective and nicer to the horse than a hearty kick and allows your leg to maintain its position. You can follow a friend's horse; when the friend's horse speeds up, your horse will need less encouragement than usual to match the lead horse's rhythm. These strategies work for transitions from slower gaits into either the trot or the canter.

To easily transition from the trot to the canter, you may try riding a small jump. As was said in the section on the canter/lope earlier in this chapter, you should work on suppleness in the trot before attempting it in the canter. The tools you will find in Chapter 6 to develop suppleness include ground poles and cavalletti. If you are riding comfortably and confidently over these kinds of low obstacles at a trot, it will be a small matter to add a raised cavalletti nine or ten feet from the last pole. The exact height will vary from horse to horse, but nine to twelve inches should be enough. As the horse steps over it, he will naturally step into a canter very easily. If not, raise it just a couple of inches and try again.

Learning a new rhythm is a prime time for bad habits to emerge, so be sure to get videotaped and/or watched by someone knowledgeable early in the process. Do this frequently so that any problems can be corrected before they become ingrained habits.

Finally, if you are having trouble maintaining a rhythm, try singing or riding to music. Simple songs are best. For example, you could trot to

> ROW row ROW your boat,
> GENTLY down THE STREAM,
> (pause) MERRILY merrily MERRILY merrily,
> LIFE is but A DREAM.

The capitalized words are the upbeat of your posting trot, and the lowercase words are the sitting beat. You can sing silently to yourself if you don't want to provide free entertainment to bystanders!

Although the canter is usually considered a three-beat gait for its three distinct footfalls, canter music will need to have a fourth beat due to the moment of suspension between strides. Or, if your horse's canter is quick, you might choose a song with a slower tempo that has one beat per stride. Of course, every horse's precise tempo is different. If you use a metronome to determine your horse's number of beats per minute (bpm), you can input that number into a music search engine for a selection of songs just for you!

# CHAPTER 5

# FITNESS

Riding is an excellent exercise for physical fitness. To the uninitiated, it may seem that the horse does all the work, but in fact riders use a wide range of muscles and need significant aerobic capacity. Professional riders are among the most fit people you will meet. A lesser level of fitness will suffice for most of us.

The age and general fitness level of the rider will have some impact on how muscle development for riding is approached. Active children build muscle quickly and easily and can usually develop the needed tone in riding lessons by riding as little as once a week. Adults and adolescents who are physically active may have enough existing muscle tone to do the same. Those who are not fit will benefit from any aerobic activity between lessons. If the heart and lungs are working efficiently, then the rider's body will be able to direct its energy into the development of muscles during rides. Additional specific exercises may be done between lessons for the strengthening of particular muscles or muscle groups, depending on the needs of the individual.

First-time or occasional riders often feel soreness in the inner thigh after their first few rides. This is the result of gripping, as opposed to balancing. Therefore, more balancing exercises should be done by those experiencing this, not more strengthening exercises.

During mounted lessons, excellent muscle-building exercises for the legs and the back include the two-point position and posting at the walk. Because these both also test a rider's balance, they should be used frequently in early lessons. Posting uses more muscular strength when it is performed in the walk because there is no boost provided by the horse's rhythm like there is in the trot. As the rider lowers herself back toward the saddle, she must be especially careful to continue to support her weight and not collapse onto the horse's back. When a rider feels the strain primarily in the quadriceps (the front of the thigh), then she is posting incorrectly from a chair seat. With the leg positioned properly relative to the torso, she should feel more like she is pushing herself up from calf and heel and less like she's pulling herself with the muscles along the front of the thigh.

Core muscles are the most important to good riding. These deep, postural muscles are the ones responsible for keeping the rider upright and stable even when the horse is anything but!

Nearly everyone will benefit from this simple exercise to strengthen core muscles: simply lie on your back with your knees bent, and tip your pelvis so that the curve in your lower back is straightened and the space between your lower back and the floor is gone. Hold this position for ten to twenty seconds. Relax, then repeat the exercise ten times. You can do multiple sets. It is such a gentle exercise that it may feel like it has no effect. You certainly don't struggle as with push-ups or sit-ups! However, a very similar movement is required in following the sitting trot, so in the next chapter you will benefit by preparing with this exercise.

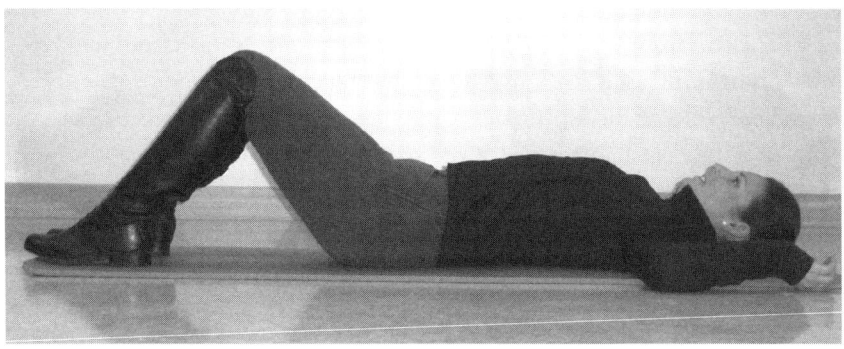

A neutral position is the starting position for many abdominal exercises.

Many riders will benefit from focusing further attention on exercises to strengthen their abdominals, and upper back, and shoulder. Fit, toned muscles in these areas will help the rider to sit the horse's most energetic gaits and to transfer rein impulses to the seat. These muscles are most easily developed through exercises off the horse. There are many familiar exercises to strengthen abdominals. Here are descriptions of a few. The beginning position of each is the neutral position.

1. **Bridging.** Using the muscles of the abdomen and buttocks, raise the pelvis up off of the floor to create a straight line along your front line, from your shoulders to your knees. Both of these muscle groups are used in a sitting trot.
2. **Abdominal Crunches.** Extend your arms and lift your head and shoulders up just enough to reach your knees. Hold the position for three seconds, then lower yourself back to the floor. This same movement can be done with a variety of arm positions.

Abdominal crunch.

3. **Knee Press.** Raise your feet so that your thighs are perpendicular to the floor. You may place a chair or stool under your lower legs for support. Press your hands against your knees for ten to thirty seconds while resisting against your hands with your knees.

Knee press.

For developing the back muscles, there are lateral pulls and various types of rows. Or try these easy exercises:

1. **Supermans.** Lying on the floor, face down, raise your shoulders off of the floor. This can be done with the arms at varying angles from the body, such as flush against the sides or perpendicular to the torso, for varying effects. Don't try to raise your shoulders too far from the floor or you will begin involving the muscles of the lower back, which for some people may be painful.

The starting position for "supermans."

Holding your arms out above your head will make you look more like a superhero than our model does, but that is more strenuous!

2. **Goalposts.** Stand with your back to a wall and your arms up so that your upper arms are horizontal, your forearms are vertical, and your pinkie fingers are to the wall. Draw the pinkies down the wall vertically. This will be felt in the muscles that pull your shoulder blades down and is a great help in correcting poor posture.

FITNESS 67

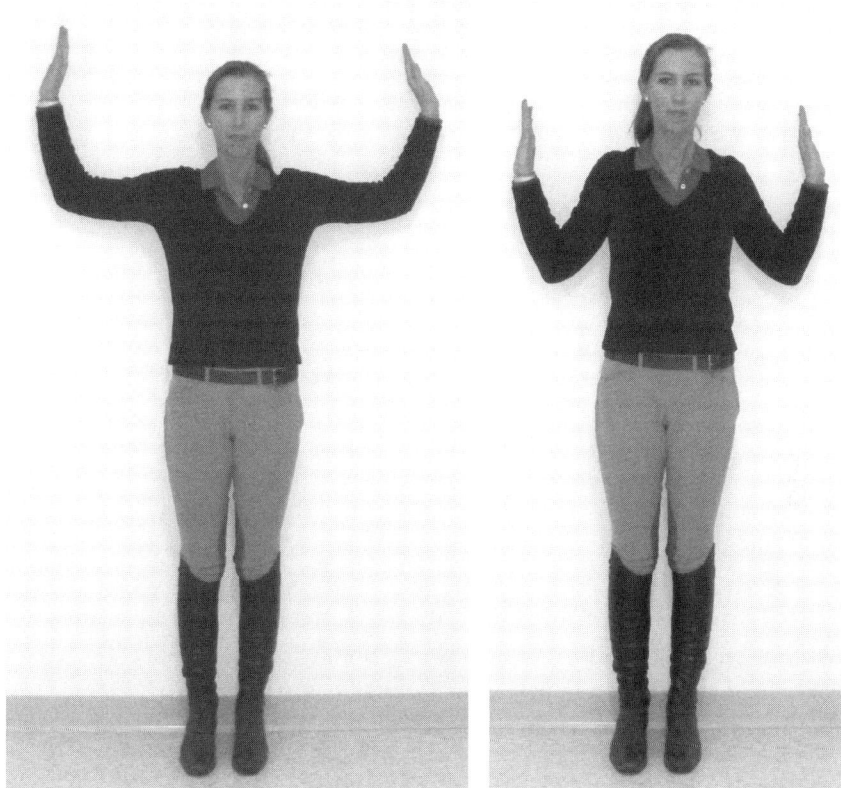

(Left): Goalpost pose starting position. (Right): Draw your fingers down the wall.

Any or all of these exercises can be repeated ten or more times, in each of three sets though you may wish to do more or less. Do what feels comfortable for you.

Building muscles takes time and repetition of exercises. It takes some creativity to keep the lesson plans fresh and interesting at this stage. Frequent repetitions of muscle-building exercises can be separated by balance exercises and mental exercises, such as locating different parts of the horse and tack and encouraging the rider to ask questions. Once the rider can perform the mounted exercises easily in the walk, her work on posting, the two-point, and other muscle-building exercises can shift to the trot. In the walk, the rider can move to the next step on the scale—suppleness.

## ON YOUR OWN

Because many of the exercises in this chapter do not include the horse, this is a relatively easy section to do on your own. As for the mounted exercises, if you are on the longe, your horse will probably be content to walk around his prescribed circle. It is off the longe that he will be tempted to amuse himself when he is bored by going a different direction than you had intended, or by sniffing at something on the ground. Just as the instructor must use creativity to keep students interested, so must you keep your horse interested if you are working on your own. Read Chapter 8, "Influence," and practice schooling figures as you build your muscles or on breaks in between muscle-building exercises. If you are muscle building in a trot or a canter, just remember to take frequent breaks for both your sake and that of the horse.

Additionally, many riders find great benefit to their riding development in seemingly unrelated activities such as yoga (relaxation, focus, stretching, and balance), Pilates ("core" strength, abdominal muscles, postural muscles), martial arts (physical balance, directed energy, posture, "centering"), and even ballroom dance (aerobic fitness, posture, nonverbal communication with a partner). Anything that improves your overall fitness is likely to help your riding. Have fun with it!

# CHAPTER 6

# SUPPLENESS

Suppleness is very closely related to balance, as suppleness is necessary to some degree to maintain balance in movement. However without some muscle strength for support, suppleness becomes sloppiness. The close inter-relationship of balance, fitness, and suppleness is one of the reasons why it is beneficial to the student to progress up the tree at different rates in different gaits. Very little suppleness is required to follow the horse's movements in the walk. However, strengthening and suppling exercises done in a walk will be very helpful to the student who is learning to follow the movement of the trot and will help her along until she is sufficiently comfortable in the trot so that she can work on suppleness in that gait. The same can be said for the rider who is learning to ride a canter; that is, suppleness exercises in the walk and trot will help her learn to ride the canter. Because of this close inter-relationship between balance and suppleness, suppling exercises are very similar to balance exercises but have the added element of movement.

The more the horse's back moves, the more supple the rider must be. The walk clearly has the least amount of movement associated with it, because there is no suspension (that is, at least one of the horse's hooves remains in contact with the ground at all times). The trot, with two periods of suspension in each stride, is the most jostling, but posting allows the rider to accommodate the bounce fairly easily. The canter frequently gives the rider the greatest initial challenge. Therefore, it is important that riders take advantage of the opportunities in the trot to develop their suppleness before expecting to be able to ride the canter rhythm fluidly.

In order to follow the movement of the horse's back, it is of particular importance that riders be supple in the ankles, knees, and hips. If they are, the upper body will be spared the need to accommodate much movement. Stiffness in any of these joints, especially the hips, results in secondary stiffness in the upper body.

An excellent exercise for developing suppleness in these joints of the leg is trotting in a two-point position. During the parts of the trot stride when the horse's feet are on the ground, the joints of the rider's legs will be relatively open. As the horse springs upward into his moment of suspension the rider's joints must close, and then reopen as the horse returns to the ground. It doesn't sound difficult, but the rate at which the opening–closing–opening must happen makes it a challenge. It is too rapid to be forced; instead, it must be allowed to happen by supple muscles. Cantering in the two-point position requires a similar movement but at a much slower rate of change; as a result, it is easier.

Opening and closing of the rider's joints in two-point.

Suppleness is a prerequisite to independent aids. Simply put, the rider must be able to use any one aid in isolation without unintentionally compensating with any other part of the body. You've probably seen young children kicking their ponies repeatedly, not realizing that the poor pony doesn't move because he's being pulled in the mouth with each kick. In a more advanced rider, this manifests more subtly, perhaps by the rider shifting her weight to the outside seat bone as she applies the outside leg to turn. The weight must match the other aids, or it will contradict, as surely as did the child in the first example.

Development of suppleness, therefore, is encouraged by any exercise that leaves the seat in position—either a three-point (sitting) position or a two-point position—while the rider moves other body parts. It is far more important for the seat to remain stable than it is for the upper body to show dramatic movement. If the rider can move only slightly without a shift in weight or position, accept it as a starting point and build from there.

# SUPPLENESS

Exercises in suppleness are beneficial to more advanced riders as warm-up exercises. These exercises can be done by the rider while she is warming up the horse, so that she can loosen up her stiff body. They are especially nice on cold winter days!

Exercises that are beneficial include the arm movements from Chapter 3 in all gaits. Also, you can do the two-point position in a trot and a canter, first without arm movements and then with arm movements.

## SETTING GROUND POLES AND CAVALLETTI

Riding over ground poles or cavalletti (poles raised two to six inches) is a valuable exercise and one that can be used at any gait. The additional bounce in the horse's gait will require an additional degree of suppleness by itself. When the rider is comfortable with the ground poles and the suppleness exercises by themselves, she may begin to do suppleness exercises, including the two- and three-point positions and various arm movements, while going over poles. This exercise adds an element of challenge to the mix but is quite strenuous for both horse and rider; be careful not to overdo it!

Poles and cavalletti can be set on a straight line or on an arc, like spokes on a wheel. Straight lines are easier to set up and to ride over. Curves are easier to longe over, and they have the added benefit of built-in adjustability: if you want to work on lengthening stride, you can simply push the horse out on the circle to where the poles are a bit farther apart rather than reset them, or you can bring your horse in onto a smaller circle to work in a shorter, more collected stride.

In general, trot poles should be set about three to four and one-half feet apart, and canter poles at about seven to ten feet apart, with adjustments made for variations in the stride length of individual horses. If the poles are being set on an arc, the horse should pass over the center of the poles; consequently, that is the place to measure. It is easier, though, to measure the ends. It is therefore worth taking the time to measure the distance between both the inside and the outside ends once they are set up well so that the configuration can be reproduced more easily. You might find that you have something like two feet between trot poles at the inside of the arc and seven feet between the poles at the outside of the arc. Precise measurements will depend not only on the length of your horse's stride but on the length of the poles and the radius of the circle.

## 72  *Training Tree for Riders*

Ground poles on a straight line.

Ground poles on a curved line.

If you are longeing over poles that are set on a straight line, you will no longer be able to be stationary. In order for your horse to leave his circle and travel a straight line, you will need to travel in the same direction and *at the same speed* as the horse. Practice these straight lines first without poles.

It is best for the horse and rider to start with ground poles and then progress to cavalletti for added challenge. Either way, be sure that you are safe. There should be no projections on which the longe line can get caught, and either the poles or the cavalletti should resist rolling. If you are using simple round poles, mound dirt around them near (not over) both ends to encourage them to stay in place.

## SITTING THE TROT

When the rider can perform these exercises with ease at a walk, a posting trot, and a canter, then she is ready to learn to sit the trot. Sitting the trot requires

# SUPPLENESS 73

a great deal of suppleness. This is why we often hear advice such as "just relax," "let your body go with the movement." Such advice is rarely effective, however, because, without muscle tone, suppleness becomes sloppiness. Following the trot with one's seat is not done by passively allowing, but by actively accommodating the movement of the horse's back.

With each step of the trot, the horse launches himself off of the ground to land on the opposite diagonal pair. If the rider tries to follow passively she will succeed only in being launched herself, landing in the saddle again as the horse lands. This is especially painful if the horse is already on his way back up again—for both of them! To break this cycle, the rider tends to focus on staying with the horse as the horse descends (gripping), when really, she must not allow herself to be launched in the first place. This means that the rider must absorb the horse's thrust with her seat, pulling the pelvis up as the horse's back rises, and relaxing and lowering as the horse's back drops.

In addition, there is the side-to-side movement as the horse steps with one hind leg and then the other. On a horse with little suspension this will be more noticeable than on one with a great deal of air time. On such a horse, the rider may need to move each side of her pelvis up and down separately in order to follow the movement most effectively. Sometimes it is recommended that riders hold the front of the saddle and pull themselves deep into the saddle seat. This can be useful for feeling the direction and amplitude of the movement of the horse's back so that the rider can then know how much she must move her pelvis to follow that movement.

As the horse's back rises, the rider must use the muscles of her abdomen to pull the pubis (the bone at the front of the crotch) forward and upward. This movement is supported by the pushing forward of the pubis with the help of muscles in the buttock and upper thigh. This action opens the angle

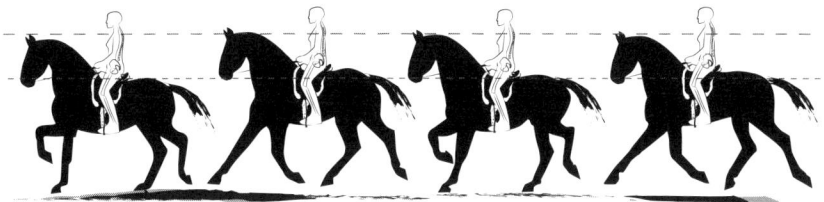

The rider's pelvis moves at the trot, while her center remains
at approximately the same height.

between the pelvis and the thigh. As the horse's back drops, these muscles simply relax, and the rider's seat lowers accordingly. Because this is an unfamiliar movement to many riders who are just learning, it often helps to have the rider sit "on her back pockets." This puts the rider's body at an angle where the horse's thrust can assist the abdominal muscles in moving the pelvis. Once the rider gets the feel for what she needs to do to sit the trot, the movement can be remembered and replicated with a progressively more upright seat.

Strength of the abdominal muscles is often the limiting factor in how long a rider can practice this skill. When the rider begins to tire, the first thing that happens is that she rounds her shoulders and drops her rib cage. The muscles responsible for pulling the pelvis upward pass through the abdomen from the pubic bone to the rib cage; this means that the ribs are the anchor against which these muscles pull when they are raising the pubis. If the rider is not sitting erect and instead is slouching, these muscles have nothing solid against which to pull to raise the pubis. Therefore, sitting the trot *cannot* be performed correctly by a slouching rider. If the rider tires, she should take a break, or move to a different exercise and try again later. A popular exercise is to alternate sitting and posting for a prescribed number of strides, starting with only a few and then increasing the number. Frequent practice and frequent breaks are built into this exercise, although a rider who is concentrating on learning to sit may not be able to count at the same time!

It is easier for many students, at the beginning, to perform the sitting trot without stirrups. It is best not to do extended work without stirrups, however, until the sitting trot is established. Once the student can sit the trot consistently, entire lessons can be ridden without stirrups, depending on the strength of the student's abdominal muscles. The work is more a test of the traits we have sought to develop thus far than it is an exercise to develop them. For example, an instructor might notice that a rider without stirrups becomes crooked. Obviously, this suggests that balance needs mentioning, but it may also indicate a lack of strength. Sitting the trot will reveal subtle weaknesses in all of the steps of the tree up to this point.

Once these weaknesses have been reinforced, the student will have a *good seat*. This is a good, solid foundation (refer back to our comparison with the house foundation). Many riders never develop a good seat. If you have made it this far, congratulations! In the next chapter, we will begin to progress upward—building the structure and developing communication with the horse.

## ON YOUR OWN

If your horse has not worked over ground poles or cavalletti before, or if you are unsure, start with one pole. Allow him to sniff it and look it over initially before walking over it once in each direction. When this introduction is over and the time has come to work, expect him to walk or trot briskly up to the pole and to step over it without altering his rhythm. The first few times your expectations may not be met, but keep at it! Get your rhythm back as quickly and calmly as possible, and go again. Soon your horse will be quite unconcerned. At this point, you may add more poles. Some horses, when faced with two poles, leap over the pair in one bound; therefore go straight from one pole to three. Again, your horse may stop and look, but try to keep that to only once in each direction to prevent it becoming a habit. The goal is for the rhythm to remain unchanged all the way around, including over the poles.

This initial introduction can be done with the horse on the longe with no rider, or off the longe with a rider, although the latter would be more productive with a ground person to adjust distances if needed.

Cavalletti and ground poles serve as strengthening and suppling tools for both the horse and the rider, plus they will reveal weaknesses in your longeing technique. If your horse stops at the poles repeatedly, or if he must add impulsion (power) to his stride to get over the poles, then most likely you have allowed him to work with insufficient impulsion all along. Develop gaits in your horse that allow him to proceed over the poles with no alteration in stride. Work your horse over poles often enough so that he becomes accustomed to this level of impulsion, and you will become accustomed to seeing it (this is called "training your eye"). It is important to have established a really good trot, in particular, before working on "sitting the trot."

Without sufficient impulsion, the horse will not be able to work through his back correctly. Without the back muscles activated, the trot is jarring and difficult for the rider to sit. The experience is equally jarring and uncomfortable to the horse, and can even cause the horse injury. On a correctly moving horse, by contrast, the back is rounded up and the horse carries the rider on a cushion of activated back muscles. Only when your horse moves consistently in a correct manner should you begin to work at "sitting the trot."

There are many ways to encourage the horse to round his back, but any that are to be considered successful combine certain basic ingredients:

1. **Engagement of the hindquarters.** Not fast, but forward. You have probably developed this through your work over cavalletti and/or ground poles if you did not have it already.
2. **Relaxation and suppleness of the back.** This is the trickiest part. If your back was uncomfortable, could you relax? Neither can your horse. If you are having trouble getting your horse round, consider that the horse's back may be uncomfortable. Some things that might interfere with your horse's back comfort include: unbalanced hooves in need of a trim or new shoes, the beginnings of arthritis in the joints, a saddle fit that is not quite right, or a rider who is not yet prepared for this level. If the rider is still occasionally losing balance, the horse will brace against her. In that case, the rider needs to do some additional work in the preceding chapters.
3. **Soft acceptance of the bit.** This is the aspect most readily seen by the untrained eye, and so many people try to create the look without the first two ingredients. Be careful not to fall into this trap. Not only will it interfere with your continued progress, it may well lead to soundness problems that will end your horse's riding career early. Acceptance of the bit must, in the majority of cases, be simply allowed, and never forced.

This is a substantial, potentially time-consuming chapter. Beginning with suppleness exercises on the flat, proceeding to suppleness exercises over poles or cavalletti, and finally, developing the sitting trot will take time and determination. If you've been riding for awhile, it may be the first chapter that you really had to stop and work at for several weeks or months. It will be worth it. Suppleness will allow you to be much safer on horseback, because you will be more capable of sticking with your horse's movements. It is so very important, too, in developing a connection with your horse through your seat and in establishing great communication with your mount, as we will begin to do in the next chapter. It's also fun when complete strangers stop to watch you ride and remark about what a great seat you have!

(Left); A hollow-backed horse, with a noticeably bulging underneck and a hollow in front of the withers. (Right): Just a stride later, the mare is softening noticeably.

(Left): And three strides later, she is relaxed, soft, and able to have her rider sit the trot comfortably. (Right): Less than halfway around the ring and again in a posting trot. The horse's head is a touch too low, and the nose is slightly behind the vertical. Compare an imaginary line along the front of the horse's face to the vertical fence post in front of her. This indicates a slight lack of energy, and the horse will again be hollow soon unless the rider gives her a nudge forward from the leg to correct it.

# CHAPTER 7

# FEEL

With suppleness established, the rider is ready to begin to communicate with the horse. As with an infant learning to speak, the first step in learning communication is to listen. The rider "listens" to the horse by feel. This concept was introduced earlier in Chapter 4 with feeling rhythm. Now this will be extended to feeling when each hind leg is landing, bearing weight, pushing, or lifting. The rider will feel for length of stride, evenness of gait, degree and evenness of engagement, relaxation of the back, throughness, and lateral bend. It can seem overwhelming, but it need not be if it is taken step by step.

Most instructors don't teach "Feel" at all, but it is a requirement for any riders who want to become truly skilled. The earlier the concept is introduced, the more readily it is learned. In fact I often introduce it in a rider's very early lessons in the walk, during breaks in practicing posting trot. It is often considered to be innate—either you have it or you don't; it can't be taught. Thankfully, that is not the case, although—as with so many other things—some individuals have more of a natural proclivity than others.

Most riders who have feel have developed it subconsciously after spending hundreds or thousands of hours in the saddle. Therefore, the first thing an instructor must do to teach feel is to become conscious of it herself. The most efficient way to do this is on the longe line, without stirrups, in a deep, relaxed seat. Just as with students, an instructor can focus more easily on the longe. Riding with your eyes closed further narrows the focus by shutting out visual stimuli. As different sensations are isolated, try putting them into words. Feeling is a right-brain activity, while speaking, and therefore teaching, is a left-brain activity. An instructor must make the transfer if she hopes to communicate this information to students later.

## FEEL THROUGH THE SEAT

By this point in the rider's education, the instructor has already begun to introduce the idea of basic feel if she has simply remarked on, and encouraged the rider to remark on, variations in the horse's way of going; for example, whether the horse is more sluggish or energetic than usual, the relative quality of transitions, and so forth. To further facilitate the rider's development of feel, there are several strategies that can be of help. One is to describe in detail what the horse's body is doing. It is best to focus on one detail at a time. As an example, explain that the horse's back will drop on one side and the barrel will swing away when the hind leg on that side is coming forward. Then have the rider tell you when the horse's inside leg is swinging. When she is able to feel that consistently, have the rider change directions and feel the new inside leg. Then have the rider focus on feeling the outside hind leg in each direction. In a subsequent lesson, you can help the student to feel the hind leg landing or pushing off. Alternatively, you can ask what she is feeling and then match one of the sensations she describes to the corresponding phase of movement. Be careful not to do too much in one lesson—one new feel at a time is enough. In fact, you may wish to wait several lessons before adding a new feel.

(Left): The horse with one hind leg stepping—the ideal time to ask for a lateral step of the right hind leg or an upward transition (transition to a faster gait).

(Right): The ideal time to ask for a lateral step from the left hind leg.

(Left): The right hind leg has just landed. This is the time to ask for a halt by closing the right hand . . .

(Right): And then the left.

Once the rider knows which leg is moving when, she may begin to compare movement. Which hind leg is taking a longer step or stepping more deeply under the horse's center of gravity? Which leg is stronger? Which direction feels softer, more bent, or easier for the horse?

When a rider is able to feel an aspect of the horse's movement reliably, she can begin to influence it. Feel and influence both range from rudimentary to an almost psychic connection between the horse and the rider; therefore, there will be a great deal of back and forth between these two steps. If all that a rider can feel is the moment when a given hind leg is lifted, she can begin to ask the horse to step laterally at that moment, making the circle larger or smaller. As the rider is able to isolate and identify more of the horse's movements through feel, she will be capable of learning more ways to influence the horse. Therefore, a rider or instructor working on feel should also read and be familiar with Chapter 8, "Influence."

## FEEL THROUGH THE REINS

When the rider can feel through the seat and legs, the path forks again. Your rider can progress in two directions: (1) learning how to influence the horse with the seat and legs, or (2) developing the ability to feel through the reins. It is preferable to teach the student to influence the horse with the seat and legs first, although the phases will overlap considerably. The rider will have an easier time maintaining the focus on her lower body without the added distraction of reins. On the other hand, having reins will open up a new range of sensations to be explored, such as when the rider adds a squeeze of the leg and feels the resultant change in the rein contact.

When reins are first given to the student rider, it will be reassuring to both her and the horse if the side reins are not altered. With the support of the side reins, the student may learn to take a steady and consistent feel of the horse's mouth and adjust to the slight change in balance that will result from carrying the reins. With that accomplished, the side reins may be lengthened so that the student may take a more active role. Finally, the side reins can be removed. Because the rider is still on the longe, she needn't concern herself yet with communicating with the horse via the reins, but she can learn to provide an elastic, yet supportive contact while receiving communication.

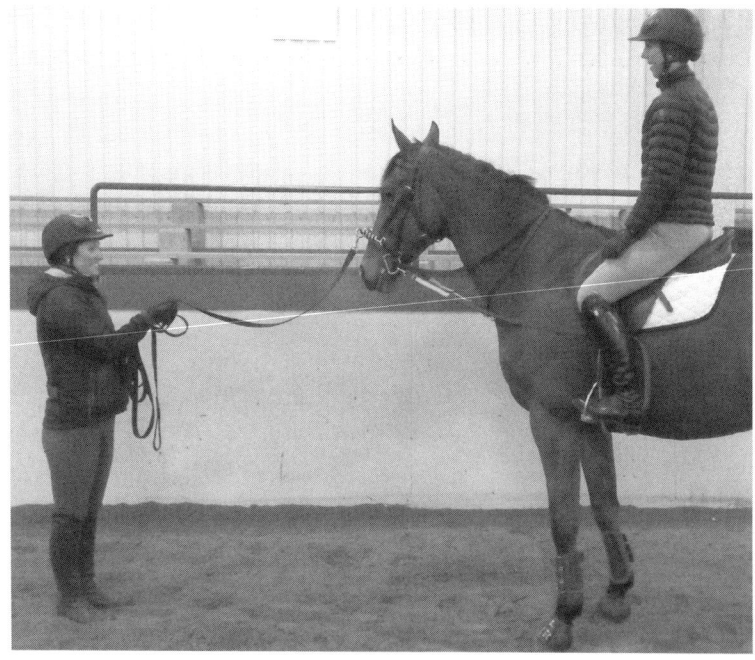

Early on, the rider rides with the help of side reins.

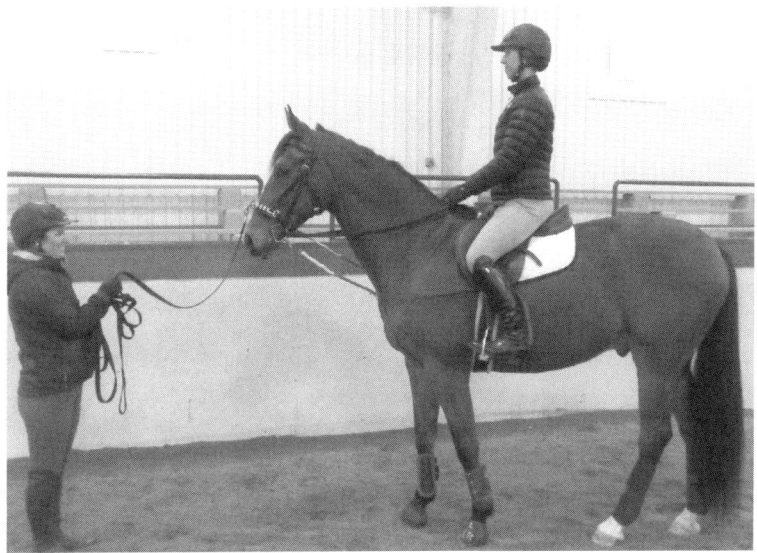

Later, the rider has reins but still has the familiar security of the lengthened side reins.

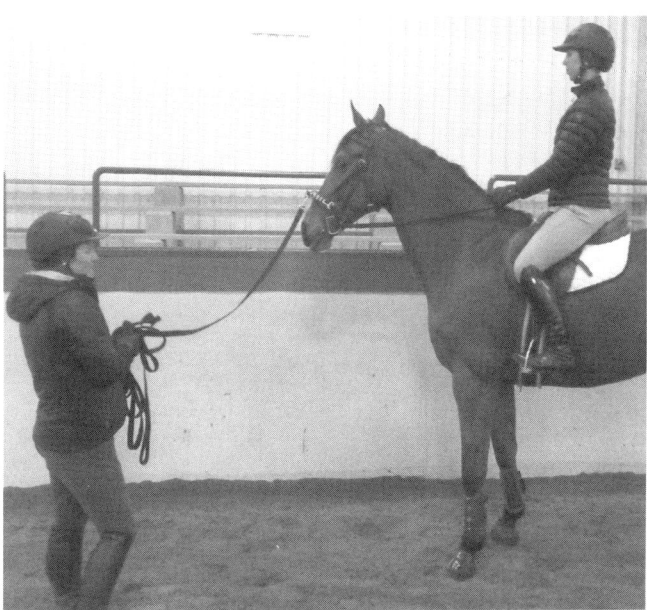

Here, the rider is ready to take a greater role without side reins.

At this point in the rider's education, the fingers and wrists should not affect the rein contact. No fiddling with the hands! The correct position of the upper body and shoulders will take on a new importance now that they support reins. Only when the breastbone is lifted until the shoulders fall back naturally can the arm work effectively. The elasticity of the rider's hand comes from the elbow and shoulder. The rider then will feel that her elbow is connected elastically to her hip, so that any heaviness or pulling on the part of the horse helps to deepen her seat, rather than dislodge it from the saddle (see page 34).

The rider should strive to feel the thrust of each hind leg alternately as an ebb and flow of the rein contact. She should soon be able to feel differences in weight or quality of contact between reins, to detect stiffness in one or both sides of the jaw or neck, and to note that the contact is "live" and constantly changing ever so slightly. All of this awareness comes from practice and from communication with an instructor or ground person who is able to help the rider make connections between what she is feeling and what the horse is doing. Remember that the rider learns about the horse's movement via observation, "listening," and gathering information that she must then interpret to understand what the horse is doing.

Once the rider has developed some ability to influence the horse with her legs, which preferably is done prior to learning to feel with reins, she should feel the effect that changing the movement of the hind legs has on the contact with the reins, and how changing the contact affects the movement of the hind legs. The recognition of this connection will be key in coaxing the best performance out of any horse, because a horse's ability to perform athletically in any discipline is directly related to his ability to engage his hindquarters and step under his center of gravity with the hind legs. Lastly, the rider should feel when the horse requires a heavier or lighter contact, which again is intrinsically connected with the actions of the hind legs.

Some exercises that will help the rider to feel changes in the horse's level of engagement include circles of varying sizes, because smaller circles require more engagement, leg yield, and frequent transitions. Circles and leg yields must be ridden accurately to have an effect on engagement. If the path is not accurate, or the horse's shoulders or haunches deviate from the path, then any potential to change the horse's level of engagement will be lost. If transitions are ridden frequently—every six strides or so—the horse will begin to carry himself in a way that makes the transitions easier to do; i.e., in balance with engaged hindquarters. These are, perhaps, easier than the previous exercises to affect a change in the horse's engagement, but expect it to take a few laps of the ring before the horse catches on and begins to prepare himself for the next transition. Be firm but not harsh or abrupt with your aids for best results.

## ON YOUR OWN

This is a tough one to do on your own. Even video won't help much, as you won't remember precisely what you were feeling when the video was shot. (You can, if you have a microphone, say something like, "Left hind pushing off now . . . now . . . now . . .," and check your results later to see if you were correct. This should be done several times to make sure that you feel it consistently in a correct manner.) Mirrors are good for seeing how the horse is moving. If you have them in your arena, you may be able to see and feel at the same time. Mirrors are especially helpful if you have enough of them to watch an entire stride. As a test, feel what is happening away from the mirror and then ride in front of the mirror to check your accuracy. Riding a variety of horses is also helpful in developing your ability to feel variations in ways of moving.

A friend on the ground is the best tool for learning to feel the horse's movement. It doesn't require much knowledge of horses at all to visually recognize the movement of the horse's legs—just a watchful eye and a willingness to help. In learning to feel the other qualities of your horse's gait, though, an educated eye is a must. For that reason, skimping on this step, or skipping it altogether, may seem tempting. However, feel is the vital ingredient that separates the really good riders from all of the rest. If you are still reading at this point, you must want to be a good rider. Don't shortchange yourself. Feel is the quality that will enable you to determine how best to communicate with your horse to maximize his performance.

# CHAPTER 8

# INFLUENCE

As soon as the rider can accurately feel what the horse is doing beneath her, the rider should be encouraged to respond to it appropriately. As the rider's ability to feel becomes more refined, she will exert a greater degree of influence. Learning influence should take place in two distinct phases: (1) without the reins, so that the student may develop the habit of responding first with the seat and the leg, and (2) with the reins, but only after a period of focusing on feel through the reins.

## INFLUENCE THROUGH THE SEAT

The rider has already learned to influence the horse to encourage a steady tempo and has been introduced to some of the ways in which she affects the horse's movement. It is but a small step, then, to learn how to aid the horse to change rhythms (i.e., to change gaits) or to influence stride length or tempo within a gait.

"Up" transitions, those to a faster gait or lengthening the stride within the same gait, are easier to start with because the rider on the longe has full access to her driving aids. At this point, the rider has had plenty of practice riding in the gait into which she will be transitioning and has ridden plenty of transitions, but the instructor has asked the horse to perform the transitions. Now the rider will learn to use her legs and seat as aids for each gait. Factors to consider include timing of the aids, strength of the aids, and combination of the aids. Again, a precise description from the instructor will help, followed by lots of practice!

The combination of aids that is used to ask for each gait will likely be the first thing taught, because it is the most necessary and consistent; however, because different trainers vary in the aids they use to ask for various gaits, particularly the canter, this is left to your preference. For example, some riders use both legs together to ask for a transition from the walk to a trot, while others use alternate leg aids because the horse's legs move alternately. For many, the primary aid for the canter is the outside leg behind the girth, while others find that a strong outside leg makes their horses swing their haunches inward; instead, these riders use more inside leg. Whatever the horse is used to will be fine.

Strength of the aids will vary from horse to horse and even on the same horse, depending on how energetic he feels, and this is something that the rider will learn to anticipate using her ability to feel the impulsion in the horse's stride prior to asking for a transition.

Timing is important because the horse can only respond to a driving aid when the hind leg being driven is not weight-bearing (i.e., swinging); however, the instructor must decide when to introduce this concept. It may be too much information for some riders to assimilate when they are first asking for transitions. Once the rider is confident, the instructor can then use the idea of timing to explain why some of the rider's requests are answered more promptly than others.

"Down" transitions will be learned, too, prior to providing the student with reins, although the quality of these may not be as consistent. Most horses would rather go slower; consequently, if the horse understands that a transition to a slower gait is wanted, he'll probably be happy to comply. The key is for the rider to do a clear transition—i.e., change, in her position. If the rider's position is wobbly, with her legs and seat sliding about, then the signal to change may be missed by the horse, lost in the "background noise" of unintended movement (and the rider should revisit Chapter 5, "Fitness"). If the rider's position is stable, then a change should be clear. To do down transitions:

**From a canter:** In a canter, the rider's outside aids should be back relative to the inside aids (see pages 50–52). To stop cantering, bring the outside aids forward so that they are even with the inside aids.

**From a trot:** Following the trot requires more effort from the rider than do other gaits, whether she is rising or sitting. To stop trotting, stop following. Don't just let go and bounce; rather, stiffen your joints so that you are still.

**In all gaits:** The rider will:

- Think of the new gait, the one into which she wants to transition, and sit as she would in that gait (or at halt).
- Stretch up and back just a little (too far and she'll drive the horse forward) to engage the core muscles.
- Give the horse a squeeze, like a brief hug, with her thighs. This interferes with the action of the long back muscles, thereby interrupting the forward movement.
- Exhale, and let her weight sink into the saddle.

In Chapter 4, use of the leg aids in the rhythm of the horse's gait was explained in terms of following the horse's movement and reinforcing the horse's tempo. With slight modifications, the same aids can be a subtle influence on the horse's gait, too. With a horse who is taking short, quick steps, a rider can use relatively long, slow squeezes to encourage longer, slower steps. With a horse that is too slow, a rider can use short, quicker squeezes to encourage the horse to quicken his step. If the horse's tempo needs to be slowed down a bit within the gait, the rider should maintain a following posture but follow more slowly. For example, if the rider is posting at the trot, she should stay in the saddle just a fraction longer. It takes practice to do this without inadvertently changing diagonals, but it is a subtle and powerful tool. If the horse needs to speed up just a bit, the rider should post more quickly. In a canter or walk, instead of using the legs in the rhythm of the horse's gait, the rider should use them just the slightest bit faster than the horse's rhythm. Another way to think of this is to ride the gait you want, rather than the gait you have. In other words, if the rider moves as if the horse was moving in the perfect tempo, the horse will adjust to the rider's tempo.

Correct timing of the aids can help the rider to more effectively ask the horse for more engagement, impulsion, or stride length. Ask with alternate leg aids as the horse's hind leg on the same side is in flight.

Lateral influence can be practiced on the longe by having the rider alternately increase and decrease the size of the circle. To increase the circle, the rider simply presses her inside leg (the one on the inside of the circle) against the horse's side as the horse's inside hind leg is swinging. To decrease the circle, the rider presses with the outside leg as the horse's outside hind leg is swinging.

## INFLUENCE THROUGH THE REINS

Having learned the extent to which the horse can be directed without reins, the rider can recognize that reins play a supportive role in guiding the horse; they are not, in most circumstances, a primary aid. Riders will quickly find, though, that reins are very effective at reinforcing a restrictive seat to slow a horse and in refining the primary aids used for direction. Riders will need to be taught the correct use of the opening and direct rein aids, as well as the possible negative effects of the improper use of each.

The direct rein aid has a stopping effect. It interferes with the action of the hind legs and stops the flow of energy through the horse's back; therefore, it is used to slow the horse or bring him to a halt. It is often misused as an all-purpose rein aid. As an example, if the rider asks for a turn with a direct inside rein, the turn will probably happen, but the inside hind leg will be less able to step under and carry its share of the horse's weight and as a result the turn will be less balanced and graceful than it could be. Because of this awkwardness, some horses will even object to this use of the direct rein by pulling back against the rider's hand or some other form of resistance. Timing is a factor with stopping aids just as it is for driving aids. The direct rein is best used when the hind hoof on the same side as the active hand has just landed; thus, bringing the horse to a halt with direct rein aids involves a one–two closing of the fists—one hand closing as each hind hoof hits the ground (see page 81).

The opening rein is the more appropriate rein aid for turns. It is the most gentle and forgiving rein aid as no backward pressure is exerted. Yet, it is nearly impossible for the horse to ignore when it is combined with a supportive outside hand and coordinated weight and leg aids. The western neck rein derives from the opening rein. The degree of sideways movement of the hand will naturally decrease as horse and rider gain skill and sophistication in their communication skills; it eventually becomes imperceptible. The spirit of openness, encouraging relaxed forward movement, will remain. The opening hand should never attempt to pull the horse sideways. In fact, if this is attempted at high speed, it may result in a fall for both the horse and the rider.

The indirect rein is also important, but it is a more advanced tool and can be introduced a bit later when these basic tools have been mastered. If it is introduced before it is needed, it will only serve to confuse the rider. The indirect rein acts minimally against the horse's mouth but primarily against his neck to push him sideways. As such, it is a key component of the western neck rein and is used in turn on the haunches and other tight turns, as well as turns away from the direction of bend. It is frequently used incorrectly to straighten a horse who is leaning in around turns where the inside leg should be used.

The best way to practice rein aids is to ride schooling figures. From the beginning, the rider must strive to bend the horse in turns, corners, and bending lines by pushing the horse's rib cage outward with the rider's inside leg. Maintaining a consistent bend throughout the horse's body over a distance is not an easy task for the beginning rider; therefore, schooling figures made up of straight lines are the sensible place to start. In these, bending is required only for a few strides at a time in corners. Good schooling figures for this level include riding center lines, quarter lines, diagonal lines, and broken (or bent) lines. As the rider becomes more proficient at bending the horse, circles can be introduced.

Accurate circles are almost impossible to ride if the rider attempts to lead (or worse, pull) the horse around with the reins. The alternative is to begin by defining the degree of bend in the horse's body and then allow him to follow that bending line until the rider straightens the horse at the close of the circle. It takes a great deal of practice to know just how much bend is necessary for a circle of a given size. The degree of bend is regulated by the inside leg, which creates bend, and the outside hand, which regulates the shoulder and keeps it from escaping to the outside. The rider's outside leg should always be further back than the inside leg on curved or bending lines so that it is not directly opposing the push of the inside leg, and so the horse's ribs have someplace to move to. Also the horse's outside hind leg is farther back, and so the rider should mirror that in her own position (see "relative straightness" on page 39).

Only when circles can be ridden accurately with consistency does it make sense to introduce figures of eight or any of the exercises that add one or more changes of bend to the challenges of circling. A demi-volte (a half-circle followed by a diagonal line back to the track) is the easiest of these exercises, because there is a significant period of straightness before the new bend must be adopted, and then the turn is only shallow with little bend required. A large (twenty-meter) figure eight requires that the number of straight strides be limited carefully, but the degree of bend is still not taxing and the rider has the entire twenty-meter circle to consider the task. When a three-loop serpentine is being ridden, the bend must change more frequently—after every half of a twenty-meter circle. This is significantly more challenging.

92    *Training Tree for Riders*

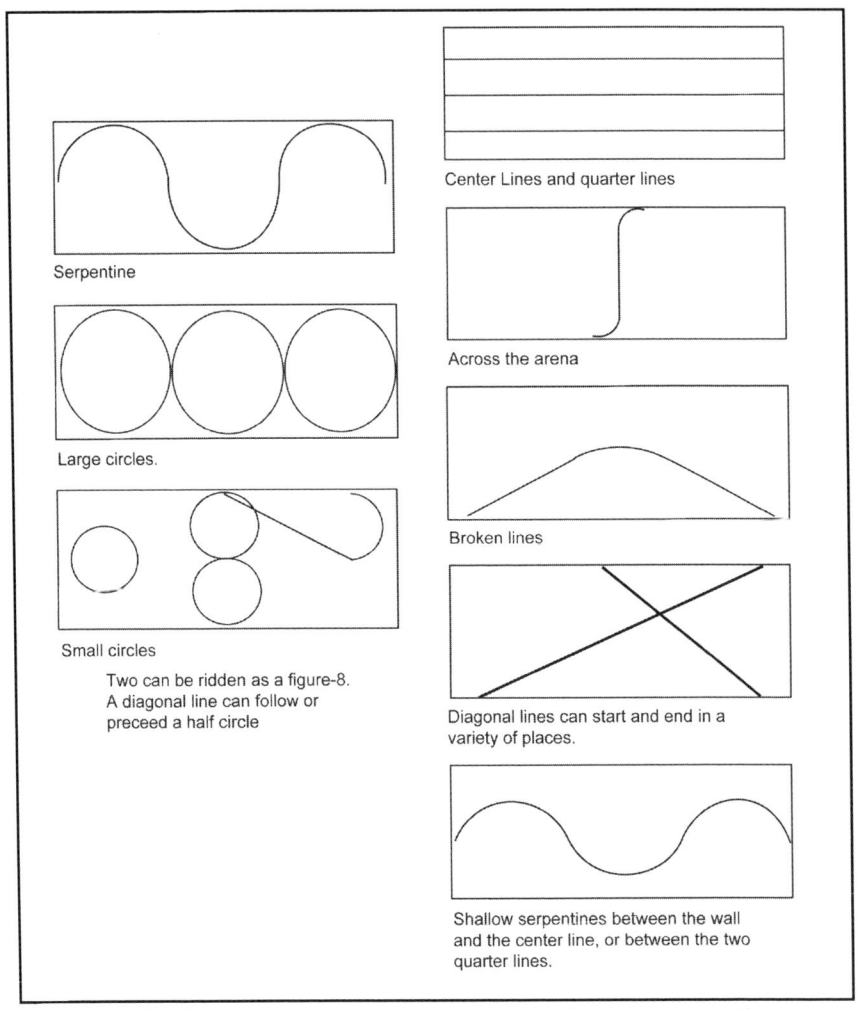

Schooling figures add variety and interest to the workout, while providing opportunities to practice important skills.

Figures in which the degree and direction of bend both change are the most difficult and will be taken on last. Examples of these are the change of direction within the circle and the half-turn in reverse. In all of these, it is important to remember that the horse must be made straight for at least one full stride before the new bend is adopted.

Because very little is required of the rider in the walk as far as muscular development and suppleness, she can progress more quickly through the steps of the tree at this gait than at a trot or a canter. And, because there will be few transitions ridden at first (just those between the walk and the halt), the rider can be given her reins, and later turned loose from the longe line for the cool-down period, quite early in the program (although it will likely be a while longer before she can advance to trotting off the longe).

With the horse in a long frame, as is appropriate for the cool-down, the rider can experiment with the coordination of leg, seat, and rein aids while riding simple figures. As the rider's skill level progresses, she will gradually spend a larger percentage of the lesson off the longe line. At first, the student will be turned loose at the end of the lesson, but once she is quite competent at a walk and a trot on her own, she can be allowed to ride the warm-up off the longe instead of, or in addition to, the cool-down period, or even ride whole lessons off the longe, focusing on cementing those skills.

In Chapter 1, "Longeing," the need to limit the length of the lesson due to the stress of constant circling was discussed. As the student consistently spends less time on the longe, the overall length of the lesson can be increased to forty-five minutes or an hour. The longeing portion of the lesson still must not exceed thirty minutes.

When the rider's skill has developed to the point that she can ride in a working frame, requiring more than a basic ability to feel and an interactive contact on the reins, she can further develop her sense of feel and timing by learning simple lateral movements, such as the turn-on-the-forehand, and the leg yield. These exercises will show the rider the value of a deep seat that allows her to feel the movement of the horse's hind legs and time the aids accordingly. This, in turn, will help the rider to understand the importance of these skills and motivate her to develop them in the trot and the canter as well.

The turn-on-the-forehand and the leg yield are closely related exercises. In both, the horse is positioned at the jaw, and there is no bend in the body; the horse looks away from the direction of travel. The primary aid for each is the active leg behind the girth. The difference between them is that, in the turn-on-the-forehand, the horse's front legs remain more or less in place so there is no forward progress, unlike the leg-yield in which the horse progresses forward and sideways simultaneously. Because the rider is spared the need to balance the forward and lateral steps, the turn-on-the-forehand is the simpler of the two exercises.

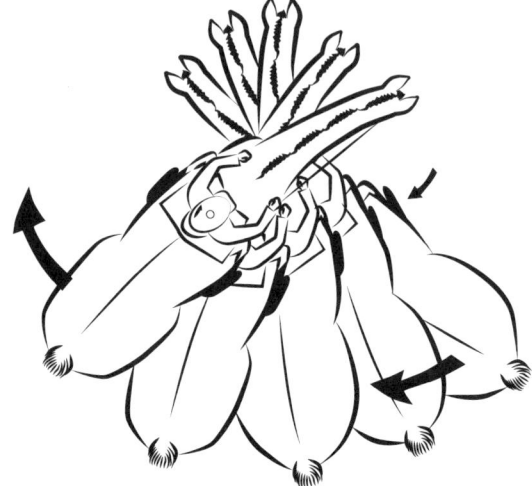

The turn on the forehand and leg-yield require very similar leg and seat aids. In the turn on the forehand, the horse's front legs remain more or less in place while the hind legs walk around them.

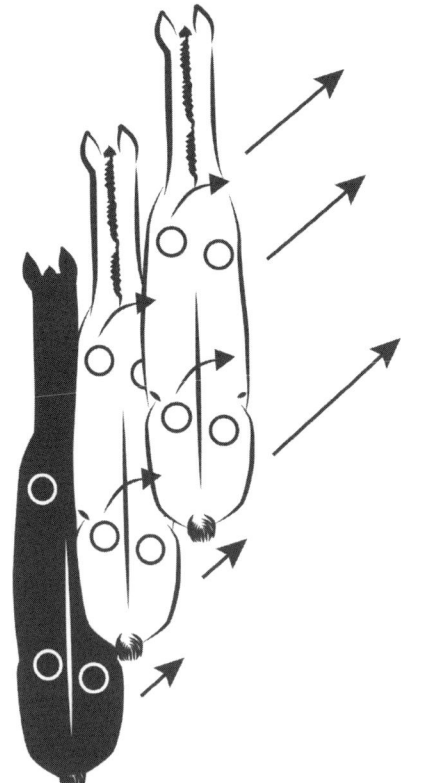

In the leg-yield the horse moves forward and sideways with each step.

To ride the turn on the forehand, the rider sits very straight and balanced and simply slides the active leg back behind the girth approximately six inches (it will feel like more than six inches to many riders!) and presses in the same slow, steady rhythm in which she wishes the horse to step sideways. It is easiest to start from a halt but also can be done from a walk. The most common error is for the rider to get crooked in some way, either leaning to one side or taking back on one rein. Either of these will prevent the horse from performing the movement. Many horses do not get much practice at the turn-on-the-forehand, and their responses are therefore slow. The most effective tactic is to be patient while the horse thinks about what the rider wants and just keep asking in the same steady rhythm, still sitting up straight and tall.

Aids for the leg yield are very similar; the active leg slides back and pushes rhythmically. The horse's first response is often to speed up in response to the leg. The rider must keep the reins short enough to prevent that from happening. Ideally, the horse makes nearly as much progress sideways as he does forward. The challenge is in finding the right combination of pushing and restraining aids to make that happen.

In the trot and the canter, just as in the walk, competency in basic figures and transitions between gaits should be developed in each gait, as well as transitions between gaits. Finally, lateral movements can be taught and obstacles negotiated.

Once the rider has reached this, the highest level on the rider training tree, she can freely choose which of the many different aspects of equestrian activity to pursue and have the foundation to be successful in any or all of them. Dressage, reining, show jumping, eventing, foxhunting, barrel racing, team penning, roping, historical re-enactments, endurance racing, trail riding, hunt seat, saddleseat, polo, hunter pacing, and more are within your ability! Specialization toward a particular discipline can now begin with confidence. Congratulations!

## ON YOUR OWN

Instant responses to the rider's aids can be expected if the timing of the aids is correct. Do you habitually glance down after a transition to check your diagonal in a trot or to check your lead in a canter? Checking for leads and diagonals can be bypassed if you know which your horse will pick up before you ask.

- Ask the horse to trot from a walk as the outside hind leg swings. The outside hind—inside fore diagonal will be the first step of the trot. Begin posting on the second beat.
- Ask the horse to canter from a trot or a walk as the outside hind leg swings. He will take the correct lead.

As your ability to influence your horse grows, you must take an increasingly active role in your development into an educated rider. You will reach a point where you know more about what your horse needs at some moments than your instructor does because you are feeling it, and feeling is richer than seeing in terms of the amount of information that is transferred. Therefore, your instructor may not always be able to tell you precisely what you must do to get the result you desire. She may, for example, be able to tell you the aids to use but not the precise amounts of each. Instead, you must experiment. Try something. If it works, great; if not, analyze what happened, make an adjustment, and try again.

As a simple example, imagine that you are riding at a trot and wish to have your horse walk. You apply the aids and your horse halts. Apparently your aids were too strong, right? So you try again, asking more gently. No problem! Riding is a conversation with your horse. You ask a question and he answers. If the answer was not what you intended, you revise your question and ask again. This "conversational riding" allows a true partnership to develop between horse and rider, as opposed to the subservience of a horse whose rider lacks feel, and is much more fun and rewarding! A riding instructor at this stage often takes on the role of translator, teaching you to expand your "vocabulary" to ask more complicated or precise questions of your horse and to understand his answers.

# CHAPTER 9

# POSITION:
# A Means to an End

The cornerstone of most rider-education programs—position—is very conspicuous in its absence from the training scale. This was not an oversight. It was done quite deliberately for several reasons. Position actually maintains a very important presence in the training scale! A correct position has evolved not just to look pretty but because it is the position in which the rider is most effective. Sitting correctly (the means) is the best way to get the best performance from a horse and to enjoy the ride the most (the end).

Any instructor, and indeed anyone who spends time observing a variety of riders, can probably call to mind a rider who, at first glance, appears very correct. Her position makes you think that the rider must be quite good. Upon closer observation, however, it soon becomes clear that the position is held with tense muscles and locked joints. The horse's freedom of movement may be interfered with. The rider has a difficult time coping with any unexpected moves on the part of the horse, and if the horse fails to fully cooperate, the rider is practically helpless.

This sad state of affairs is the all-too-common result of an over-emphasis on position. Taken to an extreme, this practice will render the mastery of any single step on the scale impossible. This is certainly not to say that rider position is unimportant. Frequently, though, when you are watching a riding lesson, you would be led to believe that learning to ride is simply a matter of "posing" on horseback. Position is often treated as an end in itself, rather than as a means to an end.

At the opposite end of the spectrum are students of instructors who focus solely on the horse. This was the case with an instructor whom I observed discussing relaxation of the horse's back with a student who was bouncing four to six inches off of her horse's back with each step and then slamming back down again. Surely if you knew that you were to receive a painful blow, you would brace against it. Can the horse be blamed for doing likewise? This is an extreme example of a common situation. Some instructors attempt to get their students to improve the movement or performance of their mounts, all the while ignoring the fact that the student's poor position is blocking the very movement she seeks. The means are ignored, and the riders and trainers no doubt wonder why the ends are never realized.

So where is the middle ground? How can anyone, student or instructor, know when or if the attention paid to position is enough, without being too much? The answer lies in the training scale, and in the end to which position is the means. Each step of the scale is an "end" in its own right. The "end" sought will be different for each rider according to her stage of development on the training scale. Early on, a comfortable position is one requirement of achieving relaxation. That position may have to be modified slightly (although it should still be comfortable) to achieve balance. Fine tuning of the position occurs at subsequent stages. Position influences *every* step along the scale.

With this in mind, you must ask yourself why you are working on position (for yourself or for your student) at this moment. What is it that you hope to achieve? Hint: If the answer is "to look good" or "to win equitation ribbons," watch out! You are pursuing position as an end in itself. You (or your student) will end up "posing" on horseback, not *riding*. If the answer is "*I don't have* to work on position," watch out! Even the great equestrians continue to work on their position daily, and you have to as well if you want to be better than mediocre.

Many instructors believe that if they teach position first, then everything else will come very easily to the student. Certainly, aspects of position are prerequisite to certain goals; however, it is not in the student's best interest to be required to have a sophisticated position when she has only rudimentary skills. The riding instructor's job is to give the student the tools that she needs to complete the task at hand, in a way that will support later skill development (in other words, build a foundation). A basic task is best completed with basic tools. The same basic task can be made more difficult by supplying too many tools. For example, an instructor can initially teach the aids for the canter strike-off as "slide the outside leg back and nudge." It won't be perfect, but it gives the student higher odds for success than would the aids (tools) as might

# POSITION: A Means to an End

be described to an advanced student: "Support the bend with the inside leg, half-halt, soften the inside rein, slide the outside leg back, inside hip forward, then scoop with your hips and lift the horse into a canter with legs and abdominal muscles together." Clearly this could easily overwhelm a green student. The same can be said for "position tools." Weighted down with rules that they cannot apply, students become tense and incapable of productive activity. Therefore, it is important for the instructor to have patience and to provide only as many tools as can comfortably be carried at that moment.

Consider the rider approaching a jump thinking, "Eyes up, leg on, soft hands, flat back, heels down, keep the horse straight . . . ." Frequently, students in this situation don't make it over the jump at all! Generally, two new things are all that a rider can assimilate at any given time. When those become second nature, the student can be given two more. This goes right along with the idea of simplified lesson plans, as discussed in Chapter 1, "Longeing." Introduce one position rule (or two if they are closely related), discuss the reasons behind the rule, and practice. If the lesson is focused on that one topic, you can be sure that the topic will be learned well.

## ORDER OF PROGRESSION

The order in which these "position tools" are provided to the student is very important. As has been discussed repeatedly, a foundation must be constructed first. The foundation of a rider's position is the pelvis. Only with a properly positioned pelvis can the upper body be supported and the legs hang correctly.

When all of the various body parts are in harmony, it can seem as though the heels are the foundation; however, in actuality, this is not the case. Consider the chair seat, probably the most common of positional faults, as one example. It most often results from the rider sitting too far back in the saddle. In that position, the stirrup bar is forward of the center of balance, and so the leg *must* slide forward. The cure, therefore, is not to pull the leg back, but to slide the pelvis forward over the leg. This frequently requires refitting a backward-tilting saddle. Once this has been accomplished, the leg hangs quite naturally in a correct position. Some fine-tuning of the leg position might comprise the content of the next "two things."

Once the pelvis is correct, then the student can move one step outward from the base to the thighs in one direction, and/or the spine in the other. When these are basically correct, then focus can be shifted toward the knee, the calf, and the foot, or toward the shoulders, the neck, and the head, progressively. Only when all of these are in order can the student be expected to hold her arms and hands, and therefore the reins, correctly.

## FORM EQUALS FUNCTION

A corollary to the rule that "position is a means to an end," and another reason to teach the standards of position progressively, is that "form equals function." The guiding question in this instance is, "What impact does this particular aspect of position have on the effectiveness of the rider?"

There are many reasons why the correct position is considered correct besides tradition, rules, and appearance. The correct position is also the most effective position for communicating with the horse. Therefore, position can be learned (and is actually more effectively learned) as a "side effect" of learning effective riding. It is no secret that information considered by a student to be useful is more likely to be assimilated and retained. By teaching the reasons for a rule of position, and allowing the student to experiment with its effectiveness, instructors virtually guarantee that no more than a gentle reminder will ever again be needed by that student with regard to that particular topic. Conversely, if a student is having trouble maintaining the correct position of a particular part of her body, instructors can be sure that the part is not performing its function correctly either.

To cite an example of this, a rider in a clinic introduced herself to me, expressing her frustration over her outside elbow. She and her regular instructor had tried for several hours of lessons to keep her outside elbow from sticking out when she was riding in either direction, to no avail. It seemed to have a mind of its own! I watched her warm up for just a few minutes while she rode some circles in which her horse consistently drifted outward, after which I beckoned her back to me. She had been giving too much with her outside hand and floating the outside rein in what she saw as allowing the outside of the horse to stretch. What I saw was her hand failing to define the arc of the circle and allowing the horse to drift over his shoulder. We then discussed the role of the outside hand in a turn. I hadn't mentioned her elbow, but when she returned to her warm-up, her circles were accurate and round, and her elbow was in position, where it remained for the duration of her ride. As soon as her hand/arm began performing the proper function, it took the correct form.

A tactic that may be useful in some situations is to exaggerate the "wrong way" in order to contrast it with the "right way." For example, a rider who tends to have rounded shoulders could be instructed to sit for a brief time with exaggeratedly round shoulders while riding the canter. Then, with an erect upper body, the rider will perform the canter again, noting the increase in responsiveness of the horse and the improved quality of the gait. Rounded shoulders are a problem of epidemic proportions in today's society, where so many riders literally do not know how to stand up straight. Correcting one's posture results in increased efficiency of the abdominal organs and can relieve back, neck, and shoulder pain as well as many types of headaches. In addition, it improves the rider's communication with the horse.

## ON YOUR OWN

If you see enough incorrect riding, your eye will be trained to accept it as normal. Take the time to seek out examples of really good riding, whether in person or on video. Analyze what makes it good, as well as what problems exist, to better recognize your own strengths and weaknesses.

Not infrequently, I hear riders complain of pain while riding. Pain from *muscles after riding* is to be expected when the rider pushes herself beyond her usual level of exertion. Pain in *joints while* riding is not normal and should not be "worked through." Most often this pain occurs in the knees and ankles. If this is happening to you, stop what you are doing and get help in correcting your position. In most cases, riders experience immediate relief upon correcting their alignment. If not, you should see your doctor.

# CHAPTER 10

# OFF THE LONGE

For any one of several reasons, it may be necessary to teach a student off the longe. There may not be a qualified horse or instructor available. Equipment or location may not be suitable. It may be a group lesson.

For students who are still working on the principles of the tree for the bulk of each lesson, the more closely the tree is adhered to, the better off the students will be in terms of solidity of their foundations and efficient use of their time. Any deviation invites weaknesses and decreases efficiency. Teaching off the longe involves a major deviation by putting the last step—influence—first. (Or almost first; if students feel particularly tense or unbalanced, they will not be able to concentrate enough on influence to learn it. Work on relaxation and balance can begin in the halt, as has been noted previously.)

## RESTRUCTURING THE TREE

The amount of influence does not need to be sophisticated but at least enough to keep the rider safe. Even the greenest of riders, then, must learn to ask the horse to walk, halt, and turn in both directions. This is usually manageable in the walk, because the lack of suspension leaves the walk smooth enough to require little muscle development or suppleness. Development of influence in the walk can, then, share time with the development of other skills. It is best for students if these other skills continue to be developed in order as much as possible. It can be very tempting in this situation to overestimate a rider's ability and push her into trot before her skills are established in the walk. This is where the first holes begin to appear in the foundations of many riders. It is important that the instructor be patient and accept the fact that, in choosing to teach in this way, she has taken a path that is longer and slower than that for the rider who learns on the longe.

Students taught off the longe can be expected to take longer, particularly in establishing balance, suppleness, and feel (see diagram on page 20). Balance will be affected because the student with reins will tend to focus on her hands at the expense of her seat. This is human nature. Every day, we perform many tasks with our hands. How often do we pay attention to our balance? Riding requires that we alter our approach to the world. We must feel through our seat and yield control of our hands largely to another being. We must let our hands be still and soft, and we must react first with our seat and legs. Before this has been learned, instructors can be sure that if they put an instrument, particularly an instrument of control, in the rider's hands, then that will be the rider's focus. The most effective way to change this focus is to put nothing in the rider's hands.

Suppleness is affected because the student will have already developed habits of stiffness, mostly associated with rein usage, before suppleness is addressed. From simple lack of awareness and lack of knowledge, the rider might, for example, collapse to the left and pull the left leg away from the horse's side as she uses the left rein. Each of us has our own demons that we fight with every ride, and most of them originated in this very way.

Feel is affected because the student will already have formed an association with the reins as her primary means of issuing orders to the horse. The rider will have difficulty: (1) redirecting her focus in order to accept communication from her mount through the hands; (2) developing good hands, because she will think of the reins as belonging to herself alone, rather than sharing ownership with the horse; and (3) sending and receiving communication via her seat. Even after the rider does learn to feel, she will tend to forget to do so having formed habits of rein usage that will be hard to break. The difficulty of teaching feel to riders who have been given reins too early in their riding educations, combined with the prevalent practice of giving reins to beginning riders, is probably the reason that so many people believe that feel cannot be taught at all.

Teaching off the longe changes the structure of the tree in that the student should work through all of the steps in one gait before moving on to a new gait. The branching tree becomes a more linear scale. Because the rider is influencing the horse in (for example) a walk—and more sophisticated influence will be required in the trot—the student must learn to influence correctly, thoroughly, and legitimately. The amount of influence that is taught at the outset is like a bandage on the less-than-ideal situation. Before the student works in the trot, which will significantly increase demands on the student's abilities, the bandage should be replaced or become a permanent fix.

A particularly difficult aspect of teaching riding off the longe is introducing a new gait. If at all possible, it is best to put the rider on the longe line at least until she has found the rhythm of the new gait. The unfamiliar jostling of the new rhythm renders the student almost entirely incapable of influencing the horse. The student's concern for maintaining control overrides her ability to feel and accommodate the new rhythm, resulting again in a much longer learning curve.

When an instructor introduces the trot, it often helps to have the rider begin posting in a walk and for the instructor to cue the horse for the trot transition as she would when longeing. In this way, the student can focus as much of her attention as possible on maintaining her balance and feeling the new rhythm. She will also have greater odds of maintaining her post and of posting in the correct rhythm. Learning the aids for the trot may come once the student can ride the trot with confidence. The student should work her way through the entire training tree again in a trot before moving on to the canter.

An excellent way of initiating the canter for new riders is to have them ride over a small cross rail. Horses who are familiar with the exercise will maintain the trot if the cross rail is small enough, giving the rider confidence. (Students should have ridden over ground poles or cavalletti quite a bit while developing suppleness; therefore, this should not be a new exercise.) After a few passes, the cross rail can be raised slightly and the student encouraged to add a squeeze of the leg. Most horses will naturally land in a canter; thus, this is an easy way to avoid the potential problems of timing and clarity of aids for the student's first attempts. The student can focus as much attention as possible on maintaining balance and feeling the rhythm of the new gait. Aids for initiating the canter can be learned when the student has developed confidence in riding this gait.

In order to maintain the interest level of the student while working in primarily one gait for many consecutive lessons, the instructor must use some creativity and planning. It is advisable to try to add one new element to each lesson and center the lesson on that, with familiar exercises in between. The new element can be an exercise from any appropriate chapter in this book: a rider exercise, a schooling figure, or a new movement; a new combination of exercises, like riding transitions on a circle or schooling figures in two-point position; or a new application for the exercise, like using turn-on-the-forehand to open a gait. Utilize ground poles and soccer cones to keep the schooling area visually interesting and to clarify where and how exercises are to be ridden. In group lessons, riders can play games or ride drill-team maneuvers.

Obviously, good riders can result from teaching off the longe. That the path is more difficult for both student and instructor may serve as incentive to change whatever circumstances require the lessons to be taught that way. In the interest of making your own work easier, I encourage you to consider that good longe horses, and good longe instructors, are made, not born.

## THE HORSE

A calm and trustworthy horse is clearly a requirement for a lesson that focuses on rider development. The less the rider needs to concern herself with the horse, the more she can focus on improving herself. Before a rider can take on a nervous or otherwise difficult horse, all steps of the rider training tree must be thoroughly assimilated.

For riders who work with such horses frequently, it is worth seeking out a quiet horse to ride on occasion. The opportunity to focus on oneself and check one's skills and habits is a valuable one. Ideally, this, too, would take place under the eye of a qualified instructor who would occasionally put the horse on the longe line and relieve the rider of her reins as well. The United States Dressage Federation recommends that even advanced riders be longed weekly.

The most difficult scenario, of course, is a green horse with a green rider. The rider needs to work on developing her own skills, but the horse isn't steady enough. The horse needs to be taught to move with impulsion and a steady rhythm, and to respond appropriately to the aids, but the rider does not have the experience to teach him. It is a combination that has been cursed and lamented throughout the history of the art of equitation. It is far preferable for the rider to put off the purchase of any horse until she can handle him on her own, but the best alternative is, again, the longe line. On the longe, the horse can be controlled by the instructor so that the horse may learn to move correctly, while the rider focuses on the progression of her own skills. With a green horse, the rider must be stronger at every step before the longe line is removed.

## ON YOUR OWN

Riders who wonder whether they've developed an overdependence on the reins can test themselves in several fun and challenging ways. With many horses, reins can be knotted and left lying on the horse's neck during a ride. Reins will be within your reach if you need them, and you can test your ability to perform various exercises (posting, two-point position, marching steps) without the possibility of using the reins to balance. You may not believe that you are using the reins for balance until you find yourself unable to rise into a post, for example, without reins.

To similarly test balance without reins over cavalletti, ground poles, or jumps, a chute can be constructed. Set your obstacles along the arena wall or fence, and then construct a wall with extra rails and jump standards, barrels, hay bales or other safe materials, along the other side of the obstacles so the horse cannot veer out. Then the horse can be ridden into the chute and the rider can drop her reins prior to going over the obstacle.

To test your ability to influence your horse through seat and legs, you can set several cones, barrels, jump standards or other safe objects in a line. Leave at least 20 feet between each. See if you can weave back and forth around them without using your reins. Leave the reins on your horse's neck for this one. Those who hold them invariably use them unconsciously! You can also practice riding circles and other figures without touching the reins.

If you are doing well with the above, an especially fun exercise is riding with no bridle. Demonstration riders do this to the awe of crowds, but it is not at all difficult for the rider who rides from their seat and leg on a regular basis. Rather than remove your bridle completely, just knot your reins and let them lie on your horse's neck, just in case you need them. Then put a spare stirrup leather, lead rope, or other similar strap around the base of your horse's neck to hold as you would the reins. This "neck rope" is standard equipment for bridle-less riders. Use it as you would reins, and it will help your horse to understand what you want from him. However, anything you ask your horse to do without a bridle should be thought of as a polite request, not a demand. You cannot force your horse to turn, stop, or slow down with a neck rope. You shouldn't be using a bridle for those purposes either. If you ask correctly, he will respond. Therefore if he is not responding, don't assume that he is not capable of being ridden without a bridle, instead try to figure out how you can be more clear and consistent so that your requests are understandable to him.

# CHAPTER 11

# WARM-UP AND EVALUATION

The rider training tree has a dual role in the rider's daily warm-up. It provides a framework of progressive tasks to warm up the rider's body and prepare her muscles for increasingly difficult tasks. At the same time, whether the rider is new to the instructor or they have worked together before, the warm-up period is an opportunity to assess how thoroughly the rider has achieved the goals of each step of the training tree. A few guidelines will help instructors and riders make the most of this key period in their sessions.

## GUIDELINE #1: HAVE A PLAN

In the case of a familiar rider, a lesson plan will have been prepared in advance. This includes riders who are "on their own"—they should always get on their horse with a plan. The plan will include warm-up exercises that the rider can do easily but that are relevant to the overall plan. For example: A rider is currently working on influence at the walk, suppleness at the trot, and rhythm at the canter. Today's lesson focuses on suppleness exercises over cavalletti at a trot. The warm-up, then, should include all of the suppleness exercises that the rider will perform over cavalletti but *without* cavalletti—first at a walk, then at a trot. This gives the instructor an opportunity to inspect the foundation that will be built upon today. If the rider passes the inspection, then the lesson can proceed as planned. The session could conclude with a bit of canter, and influence at a walk could be practiced while the rider is cooling down.

No matter how carefully a ride has been planned, one must always be prepared to toss the plan aside and improvise. If the rider is not performing the warm-up with ease, she may need to back up a step for now. Even a familiar or experienced rider will have days when she must spend extra time at a much lower step on the tree than expected. It might be that the rider is preoccupied with a situation at home or work and needs to focus on relaxation for a bit. Or perhaps the rider has some stiff muscles from gardening yesterday and would appreciate some extra suppleness exercises. To skip a step, or to dive right into the body of the lesson, might cause an instructor to miss the opportunity to notice that there is some tension or stiffness in the rider. If this happens, everyone involved (rider, instructor, and horse) may become thoroughly frustrated by their failure to achieve the expected level of performance. On the other hand, the exercises over cavalletti might be performed with such ease that they seem more like a part of the warm-up, and instructors may wish to move the student on to a more challenging exercise at a trot, or to a different gait.

If the rider is not a familiar one, then information gathered in the warm-up may be all the instructor has on which to base an evaluation of the rider's skill and to form a lesson plan. Information gathered verbally from the student can rarely be taken with more than the proverbial grain of salt for several reasons. First, people don't know what they don't know. People often think that their knowledge or skills are adequate simply because they do not know any better. Sometimes people have a vague sense that something is lacking, but they don't know what questions to ask. Second, people have a tendency to relate their most advanced accomplishment, even if it only happened once and never was replicated. People hate to be underestimated, and so they seek to impress. Third, a rider's perceptions of her own difficulties frequently do not reflect the actual source of the problems (like the rider with the unruly elbow in Chapter 9). If the rider's evaluation was correct, the problem would likely have been solved by now.

Still, a rider's own assessment offers a starting point. Whether she relates the tasks with which she is having difficulty, or those she aspires to accomplish in the near future, those tasks will form the goal of the lesson. The instructor's first task is to inspect the foundation of the goal tasks.

## GUIDELINE #2: LOCATE AND INSPECT THE FOUNDATION

Just like a house's foundation will determine its stability, a rider's foundation will determine how easily she performs on horseback. Exercises have foundations, too, the solidity of which will determine whether the horse and/or rider are capable of completing the exercise well. In general, the foundation of an exercise is formed by (1) each previously performed exercise at the same step on the tree at the same gait (if any); (2) more distantly by the same exercise at a slower gait; and (3) exercises in the same gait at a previous step on the tree. For example, the foundation of a suppleness exercise at the trot, like riding in the two-point over cavalletti, will be formed by: (1) all of the other suppleness work that the rider has done so far in the trot, like a two-point without obstacles (a previously performed exercise at the same step on the tree at the same gait); (2) riding in a two-point over cavalletti at the walk (the same exercise at a slower gait); and (3) all the other work in the trot that has been practiced (exercises in the same gait at a previous step on the tree).

Here are some more examples. The warm-up for a rider working on influencing the horse with her seat at a canter should include:

1. If the rider has already begun working on influence in the canter, then some exercises should be included. If influence in the canter is brand new, this step won't apply.
2. An opportunity for the rider to demonstrate her ability to feel and influence at the trot (the same exercise at a slower gait).
3. A test of suppleness and feel in the canter (exercises in the same gait at a previous step on the tree).

A rider working on the trot rhythm will have a warm-up consisting of work entirely in the walk, because the trot rhythm is the first thing established in the trot.

1. Review of each stage in the walk up to suppleness.
2. Posting at a walk.

If the rider has progressed to working beyond the scope of the tree, then the rider's warm-up/evaluation should include some sitting trot. In Chapter 7, it was noted that the sitting trot reveals a great deal about all of the steps of the tree through suppleness. If the sitting trot shows flaws, then these will require attention before the rider moves on to other skills. Make sure that the horse is warmed up well before the rider sits the trot so that it will be comfortable for both horse and rider. The warm-up for an advanced rider will also include work on feel and influence. Specifics will depend on the rider's chosen specialty and the intended focus of the lesson. As an example, for a lesson in flying changes of lead, the following should be tested:

1. Changes of direction in the walk and the trot.
2. Requests for canter strike-off onto each lead.
3. Simple changes of lead through the walk.

For a jumping lesson, test:

1. Suppleness and balance in two-point position.
2. Accuracy of figures at all gaits.
3. Ability to adjust the stride length.

Regardless of the ability level of the student, the warm-up is not complete until each of the exercises is performed well. If there is any difficulty with the warm-up exercises, the warm-up exercise becomes the new goal. Back up to the exercises that form the foundation of the warm-up exercise and proceed from there.

## ON YOUR OWN

Plenty of work on focused relaxation will by now have made you very aware of your body and of the tensions it harbors. Do a mental scan of your body before doing anything else on your horse! This will reveal a great deal about your level of relaxation and balance. Now proceed with your plan. The only difference is that you are the student and the teacher. If you run into difficulties, you must determine which exercises form the foundation of the one that is giving you trouble and test each of them in turn.

For example: A reining pattern requires accuracy in figures and in lengthening and shortening the stride in a canter. If shortening the stride is causing trouble, then can you shorten the stride in a trot successfully? If yes, practice that for a while and then attempt it in a canter again. If the trot stride is difficult to shorten, too, then influence in general may need more attention. The foundation for influence is feel. Can you feel the correct timing for the application of your aids? Can you feel whether your horse is moving freely? If your frustration has made him tense, you may both need to take a break. Relax, sit deeply, and focus on suppleness while you give your horse a chance to relax. This way, you'll be in the optimum position to feel and influence clearly when you start again. As the horse relaxes, test the influence of your seat separately from your hands. By continually narrowing the focus, you will soon isolate any problems and know what to work on in order to achieve the performance that you seek.

# APPENDIX 1: LESSON PLANS

## First Mounted Lesson, Beginning Rider

| Time | Gait | Exercise | Notes |
|---|---|---|---|
| 3 minutes | Halt | Conversation (relaxation) | Observe and respond to tension<br>Describe lesson plan<br>Place rider in a balanced position |
| 3 minutes | Halt | Relaxation exercises<br>Arm circles, helicopters | |
| 4 minutes | Walk | Relaxation and balance<br>Arm circles, helicopters | |
| 10 minutes | Walk | Following the movement of the walk<br>Breathing<br>Feeling rhythm | |
| 8 minutes | Walk | Simple movements<br>Stretching | |
| 2 minutes | Halt | Dismount | Run up irons, loosen girth |

Note: Times on all lesson plans are, of course, rough estimates. Precise times and specific exercises will vary with each student, depending on your observation of each student's individual needs. The above is a conservative plan. A bold student may well get into fitness exercises in the first lesson.

## Second Mounted Lesson, Beginning Rider

| Time | Gait | Exercise | Note |
| --- | --- | --- | --- |
| 4 minutes | Halt | Review of exercises; add a new exercise that requires more secure balance, such as two-point position | |
| 6 minutes | Walk | Review of following the walk rhythm | |
| 4 minutes | Walk | Two-point in walk | |
| 4 minutes | Halt | Introduce posting | |
| 4 minutes | Walk | Posting in walk | |
| 6 minutes | Walk | Alternate posting, sitting, and two-point | |
| 2 minutes | Halt | Dismount | Run up irons, loosen girth |

May provide unmounted fitness activities.

## Third Mounted Lesson, Beginning Rider

| Time | Gait | Exercise | Notes |
| --- | --- | --- | --- |
| 10 minutes | Walk | Review relaxation and balance exercises<br>Review posting and two-point position | |
| 3 minutes | Walk | Discuss trot rhythm, how it will feel, and how rider will accommodate the horse's movement | |
| 10–15 minutes | Trot with frequent walk breaks | Posting | Review relaxation and balance as needed |
| 4–9 minutes | Walk | Introduce focused relaxation, cool-down | |
| 1 minute | Halt | Dismount | Assign homework |

Homework may consist of aerobic, strengthening, or relaxation exercises, as well as learning factual information.

    Lessons will then proceed at varying rates, based on individual levels of relaxation, balance, fitness, etc. As posting becomes easier, the rider will learn trot diagonals, how to tell with which diagonal she is rising, and how to change diagonals. As an alternative to the above, riders may be taught posting first and then learn two-point position as a break from working on posting. As the rider becomes more secure, these exercises will flow naturally to riding over poles and cavalletti.

# APPENDIX 2: SKILLS COMMONLY DEVELOPED CONCURRENTLY

| | | | | | | | | | | |
|---|---|---|---|---|---|---|---|---|---|---|
| W A L K | Relaxation | Rhythm | Balance | Fitness | Suppleness | Feel | Influence | Cool-down off the longe | | | |
| T R O T | | | | | Rhythm | Fitness | Suppleness | Feel | Influence | Warm-up off the longe | |
| C A N T E R | | | | | | | Rhythm | Fitness | Suppleness | Feel | Influence | Graduation! |

# Training Tree for Riders

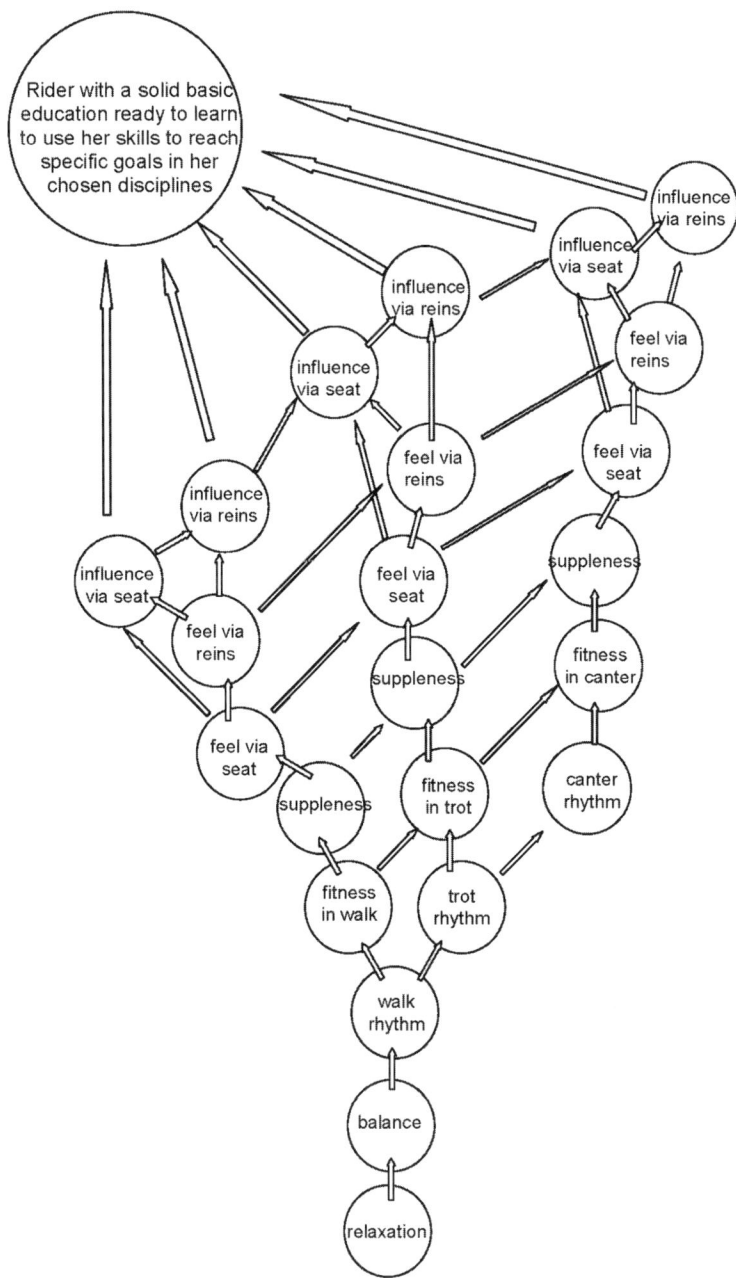

# MODIFIED TRAINING TREES  119

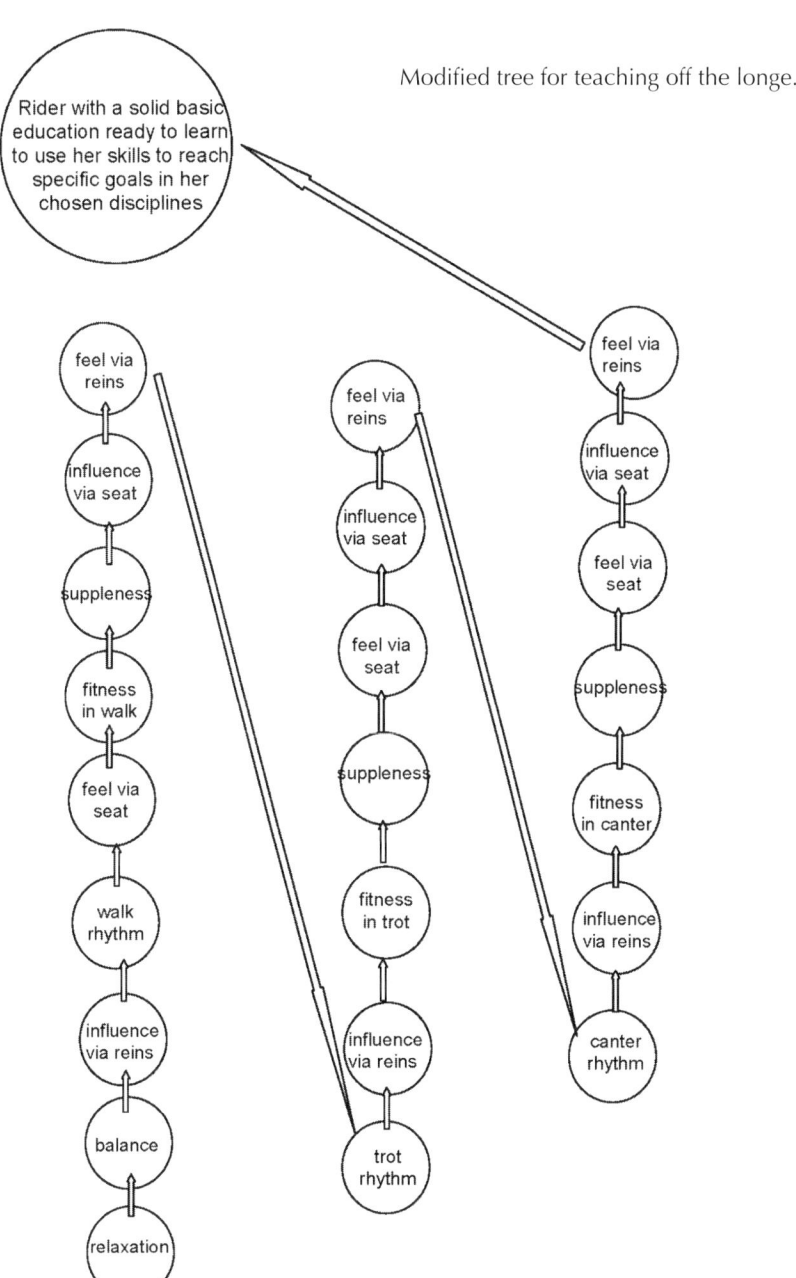

Modified tree for teaching off the longe.

# ABOUT THE AUTHOR

Amanda Berges has been training horses since 1985 and teaching riding lessons since 1988. She has experience with a variety of disciplines including Western, saddleseat, and side-saddle, in addition to her specialties of hunt seat and dressage.

Her teaching experience has ranged from children to adults, from backyard farms to national champion show stables and college equestrian programs, and in fact the concept for this book came to her while a member of the equestrian faculty at Lake Erie College as Amanda Dempsey.

Always fascinated by teaching in both practice and theory, Amanda has been certified by the American Riding Instructors Association (ARIA) for over a decade. Amanda is also a licensed teacher and a busy horse show judge and clinician. Her articles have appeared in *Riding Instructor* magazine, ARIA's official publication, and others.

# Index

advanced riders, 4, 7, 10, 25, 70, 71, 106, 112
aerobic, 63, 68, 117
anxiety, 23, 36
basics, 6, 7
bend, 15, 24, 45, 47, 48, 79, 91, 92, 93, 99
bridle-less, 107
canter, 16, 17, 18, 20, 46, 58, 59, 60, 61, 62, 68, 69, 70, 71, 72, 88, 89, 93, 95, 96, 98, 99, 101, 105, 109, 111, 112, 113
cavalletti, 62, 71, 72, 75, 76, 105, 107, 109, 110, 111, 117
cavesson, 11, 12
chair seat, 43, 44, 45, 49, 64, 99
conversational riding, 96
cool-down, 93, 117
core muscles, 23, 64, 89
direct rein, 90
fear, 16, 23, 24, 35, 36
foundation, 6, 7, 8, 74, 95, 98, 99, 103, 109, 110, 111, 112, 113
*German National Federation*, 3
green horse, 106, 107
*Heeresdienstvorschrift*, 3
indirect rein, 90
inner thigh, 21, 25, 63
jump, 5, 42, 62, 95, 99, 107, 112
leg-yield, 84, 93, 94, 95
neck rope, 107, 108
neutral position, 29, 30, 64
opening rein, 90
pain, 33, 66, 73, 98, 101
plateau, 20

posting, 51, 52, 57, 58, 62, 63, 64, 67, 69, 72, 74, 77, 79, 89, 96, 105, 107, 111, 116, 117
posture, 19, 33, 34, 35, 37, 66, 68, 89, 101
pumping shoulders, 60
pyramid, 1
reining, 95, 112
relative straightness, 46, 47, 60, 91
schooling figures, 68, 91, 92, 106
side reins, 13, 14, 18, 82, 83
sitting trot, 57, 58, 64, 65, 74, 76, 111, 112
slouching, 32, 74
Spanish Riding School, 9
spiral seat, 47
stirrups, 21, 26, 32, 33, 45, 74, 79
suspension, 53, 57, 58, 59, 62, 69, 70, 73, 103
tension, 21, 23, 24, 25, 29, 30 32, 33, 34, 35, 36, 43, 110, 112, 115
timing, 87, 88, 89, 90, 3, 95, 105, 113
tools, 62, 75, 90, 98, 99
training scale, 1, 2, 3, 4, 6, 9, 21, 23, 61, 97, 98
transitions, 14, 16, 49, 57, 61, 62, 80, 84, 85, 87, 88, 89, 93, 95, 105, 106
trot, 16, 17, 18, 20, 52, 56, 57, 58, 59, 60, 61, 62, 63, 64, 65, 67, 68, 69, 70, 71, 72, 73, 74, 75, 76, 77, 79, 88, 89, 93, 95, 96, 103, 104, 105, 109, 110, 111, 112, 113, 117
turn-on-the-forehand, 93, 94, 95, 106

two-point, 42, 43, 51, 52, 63, 67, 70, 71, 106, 107, 111, 112, 116, 117
Two-point position, 42, 43, 51, 52, 63, 70, 71, 106, 107, 112, 116, 117
United States Dressage Federation, 3, 106
vertebrae, 31, 32, 33
video, 7, 8, 62, 85, 101
voice, 15, 16

walk, 15, 16, 17, 18, 20, 32, 35, 46, 48, 51, 52, 53, 54, 55, 56, 57, 58, 59, 60, 61, 63, 67, 68, 69, 72, 75, 79, 88, 89, 93, 94, 95, 96, 103, 104, 105, 109, 111, 112, 115, 116, 117
warm-up, 2, 4, 18, 29, 49, 61, 71, 93, 101, 109, 111, 112
whip, 12, 15, 16, 17, 18, 62